BRITAIN IN OLD PHOTOGRAPHS

SOLIHULL

CHARLES LINES

SUTTON PUBLISHING LIMITED

This book was first published in 1998 by
Sutton Publishing Limited
Phoenix Mill · Thrupp · Stroud
Gloucestershire · GL5 2BU

This edition first published in 2001 by
Budding Books, an imprint of
Sutton Publishing Limited

British Library Cataloguing in Publication Data
A catalogue record for this book is available from the
British Library.

ISBN 1-84015-262-1

Typeset in 10/12 Perpetua.
Typesetting and origination by
Sutton Publishing Limited.
Printed in Great Britain by
J.H. Haynes & Co. Ltd, Sparkford.

Title page photograph: Crowned by the grand church of St Alphege – a dedication shared only with eleven other churches, to an Archbishop of Canterbury martyred by the Danes at Greenwich in 1012 – Church Hill is also 'Miry Hill'. This is Anglo-Saxon 'Soly Hill', but Solihull village is only mentioned in 1170–80, Ralph de Limesi of nearby Ulverley (Olton, or 'Old Town') probably founding a new settlement here. A Royal Charter and market rights were subsequently granted to Sir William de Odingsells who began the rebuilding of the church with its superb thirteenth-century chancel, chantry chapel and groined crypt. The dangerous footpath, shown in this early twentieth-century picture, has gone; the sticky clay, which must have concerned ancient travellers, is metalled. The road is less steep than formerly.

Aunt Sarah Jane's wedding in 1916. I am the wriggling child on Grandma Titmus' knee, to the right of the bride. Various members of the Titmus and Garfield families are included as are friends, such as the Lakins of Erdington. Some of those straw hats would soon be exchanged for other headgear.

CONTENTS

'Granny' Leeson, a famous Solihull character of last century. Approaching her 100th birthday, she expected a present of tobacco from visitors, as she was an inveterate pipe smoker. For years she was in the habit of carrying objects on her head when walking. At an old folks' party the Rector, Canon Evans, called for 'three cheers for "Granny", as she is 100 years old today'. She misunderstood, and cried out: 'I couldn't carry one cheer [chair] now, let alone three!'

INTRODUCTION

This is not a history of Solihull; others, from the great Sir William Dugdale onwards, have given us that with more expertise than I can command. Rather it is my memories of the '20s and '30s, combined with those of parents, grandparents, other relatives and friends, occasional excursions into a more distant past, or forward leap. Some writers and travellers – John Leland, Celia Fiennes, Byng of the Torrington Diaries – have tended to ignore what I still call 'my village'. Camden is unkind: 'I saw Solyhill, but in it, setting aside the church, there is nothing worth sight.' Dr Richard Pococke, Bishop of Ossory, passing through in 1757 – the year the church spire fell in a terrible storm – found it 'a pretty small neat town'. An 1840 writer says 'Solihull consists of four streets. . . . It is remarkably neat and rural in its appearance and justly excites the admiration of travellers.' Ursula Bloom's Florence Norton (*Edwardian Day-Dream*) pretended at her finishing-school, near Paris, that she came from Solihull, but 'French with a Solihull accent' which shocked presiding mademoiselles was really 'Birmingham'. A local doctor declared that 'if you want to give a garden-party in Solihull you'll need a park', reminding one of those petty musical squabbles noted in the ever-delightful Caroline Clive's Diary. A London lecturer narrowly missed an engagement because he thought Solihull was 'near Liverpool'. Another, from Brighton, perhaps under the impression that we were near the Arctic Circle, asked 'Do you get much snow here?' Grandfather puzzled me when he referred to somewhere called Silhill; it took a while to wean old residents from this, despite the best efforts of stentorian railway-porters. 'Good gracious,' exclaimed a native, 'they're not old Solihull people; they've only been here thirty years!' 'The character appropriate to the area is just departing' (Pevsner and Wedgwood, 1966). What would Pevsner think of £100 million Touchwood Court, soon to arise? Although no longer living in the Metropolitan Borough, and sometimes wishing to turn back the clock for a few hours to see the old folk, the little shops, landmarks destroyed, for me Solihull is still 'home'. But please, it's Solihull, not 'Sollyhull' as some television newsreaders think.

Any additions or corrections to the text will be welcomed. Please contact the author via Sutton Publishing.

Mother and me (born May 1913). My first memory is of Llwyngwril near Barmouth, when I was about 14 months, and seeing a train going through the little station. The journey from Solihull was allegedly made in a motor bike and sidecar without a single stop; for obvious reasons, I find this hard to believe. We went back by train. Mother, Annie Louisa Stowe (Titmus), was born in 1872, married at nineteen and died in 1962.

CHAPTER ONE

BEECHNUT LANE, HAMPTON LANE, WARWICK ROAD & POPLAR ROAD

Being 'delicate', I didn't start school till six, the mile and a half to St Augustine's from Beechnut Lane usually walked alone, there being little danger to a child in 1919. Past Grandpa's farm, splendid beech trees overhung puddles to jump over, dry leaves to kick. Nobody dreamed of a Solihull bypass slicing Beechnut Lane in two. Ivy Hall had walnut trees in a long garden. Nurse Katina Synyer emerged in bonnet from the Nurses' Home – no car or cycle – to begin her daily rounds. In Hampton Lane, a grassy 'God Cake' – so-called from those 'Coventry Cakes' children once received from godparents on New Year's Day – had a wooden fingerpost. Across the road, the Oliver Birds lived in style at mansion-like Woodlawn, earlier home of the Smallwoods, a brewing family. I was fascinated when a neighbour's 'help' told me that 'Mrs Bird puts on a hat for her lunch and rings the bell for the parlourmaid to bring in the next course.' (Ladies wearing hats at their own table must be as rare now as parlourmaids.) Calendar-pretty Ivy Cottages were at School Lane corner by the former Martha Palmer Charity School. At Warwick Road, Maid's Cross had a gate into an unscathed Malvern Park.

A bluebell spinney graced the New Road, Warwick Road junction. I usually kept to the latter road, wishing Father would buy a 'monkey-puzzle', like that in Mr Archer, the architect's garden at Park Dene, possibly saw a Birmingham-bound 'bus with solid tyres, gas-bag on top, saving petrol. Beyond Georgian Bradford House, I envied cadets who might be entering what we still somewhat incorrectly called the Grammar School. Opposite was a house, once a young ladies' school attended by Mother and her sister. (This establishment was conducted by the Misses Edwards, 'an Admiral's daughters', one was told, though he died as a Commander. Poor as mice, they could, however, claim descent from local Holbech, Mashiter and Short families of esteem.) Existing houses in George Road were out of sight on early walks; one saw only weedy footpaths, rusty street lamps, neat allotments. Near the old Tanyard was Mrs Thornley's substantial house, Broomfield, built by Charles Madeley who had managed the tannery for his widowed mother. Two Thornley daughters, spinsters, always sweetly smiling, never seemed to grow a whit older through the years. Schoolmasters lived in gloomy villas by the Congregational Church flanking Drury Lane and Teinter's Green, an open space where newly woven cloth would be hung to dry on 'tenterhooks', when this was a Solihull industry.

Grizzled tramps waited of an afternoon by the old Golden Lion for the Union workhouse to open. Between Drury Lane and Mill Lane, Arthur Sidwell's pork-butcher's shop might be half-concealed by its proprietor. (Arthur weighed 31 stone. A Birmingham tailor advertised very cheap suits to measure, but wouldn't let him have one.) Nearby, Basford, the saddler, Heelis, the red-faced vet, the latter always smart in breeches and leggings, acrid smoke from the blacksmith's.

I passed Mill Lane's cottages and few shops. This also had the Church of England Boys' School with dreary playground and the telephone exchange which was located in somebody's front-room. That exchange was the bane of my father's life; he alleged that the operators – supplanted by the householder herself at weekends – spent their time knitting and gossiping instead of answering his calls.

On the main road (here sometimes called Golden End, a name given to markets as at Knowle) rabbits festooned Aldington's shop, haughty young ladies presided at the 'new' post office of 1911. The Infant Welfare had a rocking-horse in the window, a crippled tailor sat cross-legged near the 'clock shop', where little Arthur Hobbins opened shutters at nine, a big timepiece telling me I was getting late for school. You wouldn't get a cheery word from this Arthur, or William Chinn, the butcher and grumpiest of men, though you might well from dear Dr Whitehouse hard by. At the Barley Mow crossroads, a policeman would be on point-duty, eventually replaced by an RAC man in brighter hue. Round the corner in Poplar Road, Lloyds Bank and the Public Hall neighboured the police station. Two charming old houses were adjoined by the long-secret garden wall of Silhill House.

George Lines, my father (1862–1944), was born at Lea Hall, Yardley, a Yardley of winding lanes and dog-roses, corn stooks and whistling ploughboys. His father hailed from Chipping Warden, Northamptonshire, where forbears can be traced back to the seventeenth century. Father left school at ten (save for night school) and worked with his uncle, William Henry Powell, pump-maker, well-sinker and farmer, of Hillfield Farm, Homer House, in Blossomfield, and Lower Trinity Street, Birmingham. He spent some time (briefly) in Canada and London before setting up for himself in his uncle's line at Church Hill and then High Street, Solihull. He married in 1891, Mother's family a bit 'uppish' with landed gentry as cousins, but doubtless regarding him as a coming man. Like many more or less self-made men, he could be a hard employer, and wouldn't be invariably popular today! He loved his garden, taught me to read, although he never read many other books, but did read two newspapers daily, showed me the Warwickshire and Worcestershire countryside, hated cigarettes, but would put his pipe in his pocket and often set himself alight. . . .

Mother with my eldest brother, William George (1892–1966), who figured in a church window designed by Joseph Pippet of Lode Lane, but no one seems to know where this is. Engineer, water-diviner, local councillor and Rotarian, he served in the Army in the First World War, and in Rescue Service in the Second, and, with my youngest brother, Harold Henry (1903–77), succeeded to the family business. This has now been sold.

With prosperity dawning, my parents left High Street and built Linehurst between Solihull and Elmdon Heath. Friends asked anxiously, 'Why are you burying yourselves in the country?' True, in the last century, there was no gas here, no mains water, of course no electricity, and until about 1920 no telephone. Yet apart from Father's workmen (as many as sixty or so at one time), there was plenty of activity – errand boys, coalmen, chimney-sweep, piano-tuner, my sister's music-teacher, the baker from Catherine-de-Barnes with sweet-smelling loaves, occasional hurdy-gurdy men, knife-grinders and 'any old iron?' I remember a telegraph boy arrived the very moment maroons sounded in November 1918, and subsequent ex-Servicemen with pathetic little bundles of shoe-laces. We didn't go to the doctor: he called. Tramps begged hot water and 'a pinch o' tea, mum'. 'Salty' Nance appeared with horse and cart and blocks of salt for the home-cured bacon I detested, making an inevitable attempt to purloin the backdoor mat and requesting 'a piece of cake for the little lad, he hasn't had any breakfast this morning'. He never grew older, and was no more existent than Dickens' celebrated 'Mrs Harris'. Straying cattle and sheep were decidedly unwelcome when a gate was accidentally left open. A Christmastide band, ostensibly playing for 'charity', received a whole shilling from Father, who was not pleased to find that it was spent later at the Greville Arms nearby, and he didn't care for carol singers with their 'goo' Kin Wenslus', and hammering on the door. More welcome (always with an oil lamp after dark) were the two postmen for their annual Christmas box, although some people were cross when Saturday deliveries were reduced to two, 'so that they can go to football matches, if you please!' There might be the carriage from Elmdon Rectory, a traction-engine, steam roller, the North Warwickshire Hunt, and when 'the lights' were on again, the lamp-lighter with long pole. Schoolchildren from the 'Heath' chattered by; so did their mothers, in laced-up boots, who 'obliged other ladies'. And there was the man with one leg rather shorter than the other, unkindly called 'dot and carry one'.

  The villas to the right were built by Father before the First World War.

The house, my parents' pride and joy, now signified simply by two large oak trees, was large, with high ceilings, draughty and made much work for loyal 'dailies'. The dining room easily seated a dozen round an extended table. Mother spoke of twenty-six for Christmas dinner (two sittings), a ritual partly terminated, I fear, by that rift over Great-Aunt Sarah's will which reduced the number for Christmas walks over the fields and inspection of ricks. Year by year, the drawing room retained that satin-striped wallpaper with rows of tiny flowers, half-concealed by pictures that included 'Bubbles' and 'Cherry Ripe', and a host of family photographs, some of them in this book. Floral carpet, floral mahogany chairs, gasolier when lamps were abandoned, miscellaneous ornaments — why did I persuade Mother to give away those vases with hanging drops? — all made a setting for parties with very amateur conjuring, ghost-stories, cards (never on Sundays), early wireless, 'Indian Love Lyrics', songs about 'bravely rolling ships' and sailors lying on the ocean bed, but not 'Close the Shutters, Mollie's dead'. Domestic regions were quarry-floored, with a big range to blacklead, pantry steps, bacon-rack, thralls for milk-pans and beer barrels. A bathroom was added after some years. The garden, edged with many yards of hawthorn and holly, supplied innumerable wants including lots of fruit for preserving. Tennis court and paddock provided recreation, and there was shooting for Father and farmer brother Frederick, Yew Tree Farm having been bought. Three brothers went dancing, always with white gloves.

A large wicker basket in the Linehurst laundry spoke of family holidays at Weymouth, Ilfracombe and Aberystwyth, but that was before my time. For years there was little thought of going abroad (such 'foreign messes', even 'black bread' and Spain just bullfights and oranges). Father talked of his visit to Canada, but that was 'business'. My few days in Paris from Wellesbourne House School were 'educational' (a bit more educational than parents imagined). Cousin Arthur and Lizzie went to France for a day and found an English café and boiled ham — no frogs or horsemeat. Auntie 'Tot's' friend Lilian spoke of 'that heat and dust', as if the Tropics began at Calais. After many countries, I think fondly of lunching in Wethersfield, Connecticut, with Richard and Evelyn Griswold, their home named after Warwickshire-born seventeenth-century Michael Griswold who, with others, crossed the Atlantic for religious reasons. (In Solihull we think 'Greswold'.) In Richmond, Virginia, I stayed with Throckmortons, proud of their distant links with Coughton Court and one-time lords of the manor of Solihull; about eighty Throckmorton entries in the local telephone directory there, and both names are widespread in the United States.

Above: Grandpa John Titmus, Grandma Titmus, Auntie 'Tot' (Sarah Jane), Mother and uncles William and Harry, c. 1890. Mother has very short hair, apparently a fashion of the day, if much deprecated by Auntie, who declared she would 'like to be the last woman in the world with long hair'. Mother said: 'then they'd put you in a circus!' Auntie christened their little farmhouse Elm View, because it was mistaken for The Cottage, also in the lane – and not a cottage at all!

Father's mother, Elizabeth Powell (1833–1905) from Herefordshire. She had a reputation, as a widow, for carrying tittle-tattle from one relative's home to the next. One of her brothers was 'Pumpy Powell', the well-sinker and pump-maker; another made a fortune in Toronto. A grandson, sent out to live with him, refused to sweep snow outside the house, seriously disappointing family expectations. Her daughter, Emily Pearson (1868–1905), emigrated to Coburg, Ontario, husband Joseph utterly refusing to believe that photographs of a far from rural Yardley, taken after the Second World War, were genuine.

Grandma Titmus (Lucy Stowe), aged fourteen and wearing a gingham dress, 1857. One recalls her in bonnet, black and jet, afterwards bedridden, but still with a host of stories – Warwickshire Yeomanry camping in Elmdon Park, the walled garden there with its luscious fruit, men mowing their own fields by hand from four in the morning 'before they went to work'. An elm outside her bedroom window obscured the view: if she'd had her health, she said she would have dealt with it – a hint of witchcraft, perhaps?

My great-grandmother Ann Birch, born in 1825, married Joseph Stowe, from Bugbrooke, Northamptonshire, in 1838. He was a Solihull shopkeeper. I gather it was she who had the habit of taking a warming-pan to bed after her husband had retired. One night she filled it with ice and he screamed, 'I knew you'd burn me one of these days!'

Mother would hardly remember her mother in a crinoline, as seen here, but told me of playing with the discarded hoops of a potentially dangerous garment; also of a woman whose bustle waggled absurdly as she walked along High Street! Talking of fashion, Mother ordered a 'Newmarket Coat', then all the rage after famous Vesta Tilley ('Burlington Bertie') wore one in a Birmingham pantomime.

Auntie 'Tot' (Sarah Jane), rather the 'belle of the ball' when young, adored dancing and music, sang, loved flower-arranging, cookery and painting in oils, indulged in a little millinery, aspired to be nurse or 'lady gardener'. She said she 'always kept clothes until the fashion came round for the third time'. It didn't quite work out. Married to a much younger husband, she surprisingly settled down to looking after ageing parents, milking the cows, tending poultry and pigs. Fortunately, she found time to tell me lots of local scandal, such as that of the 'Malvern Hall murder' (which didn't happen, at least not at Malvern Hall), and a certain family 'tin-kettled' out of a neighbouring parish for ill-behaviour. There was also the tale of the Elmdon Hall cook who, if taking a dislike to a maid, would allege that the girl had stolen some item of silver. At Cook's demise, her own box was found to contain an interesting collection of silver. . . .

The little farmhouse, later Elm View, ivy-clad and primitive in many ways, with a circuitous walk to the pump, fascinated me. A longcase clock had phases of the moon on its dial; there was wax fruit under glass domes. Candles and lamps sufficed until gas was belatedly installed, I think after Grandma's time. Hot bricks from the kitchen range served as hot-water bottles, Auntie decorated a spare room with pictures cut from magazines — some of the film star, Rudolph Valentino, whom she adored. Several fields had old and rare apple-trees in the hedges, the garden had an arbour for tea parties, and there were sweet williams which Grandpa loved. Better than tea parties was when Mother (a father's child) accompanied my grandfather on a job mending fences, and they had lunch of bacon and eggs fried on a clean shovel. A picnic on the Malvern Hills included a donkey ride on a narrow footpath, which she didn't like owing to the precipitous path. A carpet bag containing the family lunch was found to be locked, the key left at home, and it had to be broken open, with some difficulty. In this picture Grandma (left) and Auntie are behind the gate, with uncles William and Harry.

Great grandmother Louisa Limbrey, or Limbery, born at Lyme Regis in 1815, married Jacob Titmus, builder and shopkeeper, in 1838. She looks a formidable character and one fancies it was she who caused the satin dancing shoes to be returned (see p. 36). A daughter, also Louisa, made children 'sit up straight' and carefully mind their manners.

Elm View has been completely – and most attractively – transformed since I lived nearby. Gone are the fields of memory, the summer arbour and Grandpa's sweet williams, and Beechnut Lane is now built up and divided by a bypass.

Elm View as it is today, transformed by Mr and Mrs J.E. Goodchild, the present owners. John Goodchild is a well-known architect.

G.A. Martineau described Beechnut Lane as 'one of the most beautiful sights of Solihull, being lined from end to end with its glorious beech trees'. Actually, this only applied to the upper part of the lane. Father, Mother, my sister and a brother appear on this picture postcard of about 1908.

The upper part of Beechnut Lane, 1997. Greenery conceals the many houses now lining it, the road in much better condition than in the early 1920s. Father objected to its state, writing and complaining to the Rural District Council.

Ivy Hall, corner of Beechnut Lane and Hampton Lane, the Feltons' old home in my day, had a Georgian entrance-front masking earlier black-and-white work, a great loss. The Pearsons were there in 1874, and Ann Briscoe, farmer at Ivy Hall farm.

The Ivy Cottages, corner of Hampton Lane and School Lane. Was an architectural survey conducted; could they have been restored? There were nice, old-fashioned gardens and the roofs were thatched at one time as this photograph shows.

Maid's Cross, doubtless named after some unfortunate maiden buried at the crossroads, and once called Maid Good's Cross. Deebank's Cottage disappeared in about 1895. A gate led into Malvern Park, where Grandpa took me to Sanger's Circus with its delights of Pimpo the clown, 'Red Indians' chasing a burning coach, Japanese acrobats, elephants and a tightrope walker not venturing very far from the sawdust.

Bradford House, Warwick Road. Richard Bradford Thompson built it as a boys' school in 1799. In 1858 William Robertson, Birmingham dental surgeon, bought the freehold property, 9 acres, for £2,000, retiring there in 1866, dying in 1870. Two of his eight children, Mary Ann and Martha Felicia ('Flitty'), lived at Bradford House until 1914, dying within hours of each other. Mary Ann wrote a charming book of poems, sumptuously bound. 'The colourful bonnet-strings of their Sunday headgear were the wonder and admiration of my young eyes,' wrote one who knew them. They rang a little bell to announce feeding-time for the birds. Small boys fighting outside the gate worried the sisters. Bestowing coppers to stop these fierce battles, the poor dears never realised that these were 'stage fights', producing a useful income for the youngsters. Little Annie Deebank (see p. 73), employed to weed the garden path, was to receive 1½d. A penny was produced, and she was told to return for the halfpenny, but this was refused, one sister saying: 'Never crave for money, it's the root of all evil!' Solihull United Charities bought Bradford House in 1921.

Solihull School, formerly Solihull Grammar School, dates from the mid-sixteenth century (this picture is *c.* 1900), but only opening on its Warwick Road site in 1882, with designs by J.A. Chatwin who – judging from a catalogue of his architectural work here and elsewhere – must have burned quantities of midnight oil in his time. Since then it has undergone periodic enlargement, not invariably of the best quality, though an exception must be C. Neville White's chapel by Maid's Cross. The achievements of Dr Robert Wilson (headmaster 1879–1908, and later Vicar of Tanworth-in-Arden), first at the ancient building near Solihull Church, make far happier reading than the huge list of complaints about the establishment submitted by Solihull people in 1850. Today the school has a good academic record.

Meeks' cottage, Warwick Road. Our boots and shoes were collected, repaired and delivered from this now vanished cottage which had some pretty Gothic features. It was probably an adjunct of the nearby tanyard.

The Tanyard (opposite the Little Tanyard) was established by John Madeley and afterwards managed by his son, Charles, on behalf of his mother (a Harborne) at Touchwood Hall. After closure in about 1867, the industrial buildings were converted into dwellings. Charles built Broomfield hard by as a residence for himself. All are now demolished.

Drury Lane, earlier Dog Lane, after demolition. Strolling players, performing in a barn, are said to have inspired the change of name, but Father continued to say 'Dog Lane', and told me he could remember when it ran through the Touchwood Hall farmyard, with gates to be opened and shut at either end. The Victorian Congregational chapel has also disappeared, replaced by Christ Church, north of Warwick Road.

The Church House, Drury Lane, established in the nineteenth century under the aegis of Canon Evans, Solihull Rector, was used for church functions, Sunday Schools (naughty boys in the corner) and the Carnegie Library, books on trestle tables. Caretaker Mrs Brown served hot soup to Drury Lane needy in winter. The photograph was taken after sale for business premises.

The Drury Lane of today under construction. Everything of 'Dog Lane' has gone from Touchwood Hall to the Church House and the cottage of White, the pig-killer, who arrived for his 'executions' well after a sojourn in licensed premises.

A victim of the Mell Square development, Touchwood Hall dated mainly from about 1712, but was on a much older, once moated, site. The Geoffrey Martineaus – Mrs Martineau was Charles Madeley's daughter – kept their front door ajar in daytime, for passers-by to step in and rest, a kindly gesture eventually featured in an American newspaper.

The interior of Touchwood Hall, Drury Lane, while the Martineau family lived there. The chimney-piece is now in the Manor House.

Solihull's second workhouse (the first nearer the Barley Mow) was much larger than one might suppose from this Union Road view. Demolished a few years ago, it was built in about 1836 by Harper of Tanworth who was reputed to have made a profit of £800 over the transaction – not bad for the time. The infirmary and the recent big hospital were added later.

In 1845 Rector Archer Clive and Colonel Short, as magistrates, fined a chimney sweep £10, or four months gaol, for brutally assaulting a boy who had been sent up chimneys. The child was sent to the workhouse where he 'clung to the Master of it and finds himself in a state of Luxury of which he had no conception' (Caroline Clive's Diary).

Replaced between the wars, the old Golden Lion, pictured in about 1900, welcomed some of the passing coaches. Scratched on a window-pane were the words: 'Thomas Sorter, officer of Excise, Birmingham, bolted with A. Bellamy, Miss Lucas, Miss Jones, 1780. £2,634 – 19s.6d.' The *Knowle Journal* commented: 'whichever was the name the lady was christened in, she was equally valuable from a monetary point of view, and in the face of handling £2,634 odd the officer was content to "bolt" and ask no questions regarding his charmer's legitimate name.' The inn was long associated with the Capner family, one a member of the local Troop of Horse raised during the Napoleonic threat.

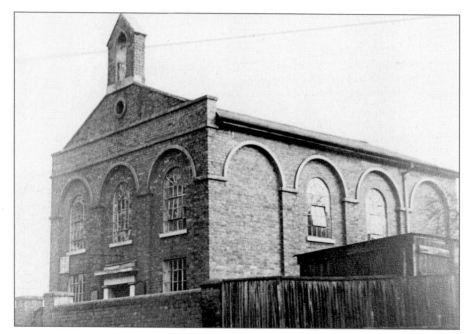

Once complete with clock and bell, this one-time Independent chapel (Bethesda) was built in 1826, before the building of the Congregational church in Warwick Road. It was used for Sunday schools and various functions. Now replaced by the John Palmer Hall, it would have made an excellent little theatre. Both churches have been demolished, and a new Christ Church has now been built.

Destroyed in the making of Mell Square, this timber-framed 'hall house' was a feature of Mill Lane. What a pity it was not dismantled and rebuilt elsewhere, Avoncroft Museum of Historic Buildings perhaps.

Old Mill Lane's Rima Café, earlier home for many years of Mr and Mrs George Pegg, my sister's parents-in-law, and their daughter, Phyllis (Mrs Raby), of the well-known Raby Trio of musicians. An old-fashioned garden extended towards Drury Lane. Mill Lane was known for a time in the nineteenth century, confusingly, as New Street. The mill and pond disappeared long ago.

The Hawthorns, Warwick Road, became Solihull's post office after High Street closure in 1911. As a private house it had been the home of Mrs Heaton, mother of Mrs William Upton of Sutton Grange and Berry Hall. Mrs Heaton was not at all pleased when she discovered, on belated inspection, that her coachman was in the habit of washing only one side of the carriage – 'put the carriage away, James, we shan't be going out today' – but I'm not sure if he was dismissed.

The former Warwick Road post office building still exists, having subsequently served various other purposes. First transferred to Station Road, the office is now in Mell Square, near 'Windy Alley', as some folk term part of the new Drury Lane.

Mrs Aldington (right) outside her Warwick Road shop (fruit, vegetables, fish, poultry). Rapidity in skinning rabbits would today earn her a place in the *Guinness Book of Records*. A great worker for the local Methodists (and apt to pour half-cups of tea at functions), she lived to be a centenarian. An earlier shop was just at the Warwick Road – Mill Lane corner.

Edward Hobbins, clock and watchmaker and jeweller, outside his Warwick Road premises before the First World War. The shop was almost certainly that of James Wells, who, in 1819, supplied a new clock for Solihull Parish Church at 100 guineas. This was to show quarters, hours and minutes, have a copper dial 6 ft in diameter, figures and hands well gilt. Edward Hobbins' daughter, when not in her first youth, married a cousin, Frederick Forder, who had come over with the Australian forces in the First World War. He sailed for home, promising in loving letters to send for her, and provide a beautiful home, but never did, a mystery unsolved. She told people, 'He's in the Bush.' I recall her on the front doorstep in a hat with a large rose, perhaps the very one she was married in. The picture below was taken many years later. This projecting shop has now gone. I remember it as Hassall's, later Bramwell's, as here. Arthur Hobbins succeeded his father.

Dr E. Sutton Page, shown here, retired to this Warwick Road house, later part of Rogers' Garage. 'Bills, bills,' he used to say, 'you know what to do with bills, chuck 'em on the fire! Know what to do with cucumber? Put plenty of salt and vinegar on it, then throw the whole beastly lot in the dustbin!' Doctoring in Solihull has quite a fascinating history. Dr John Short, born in 1740, was succeeded at what we now call Quinet House by his son, Dr Richard Short. The latter died in 1837, after being joined by Dr Thomas Lowe, who died in 1883. Lowe was joined in about 1860 by Dr E. Sutton Page, who scratched his name on a window pane, and was the builder of Sutton Grange (now vanished) in Station Road. The practice passed in 1890 to Dr A.V. Bernays who was to be joined by Dr Whitehouse. The Page dynasty endured for three generations, via Dr E. Ferdinand Page (d. 1944) who lived at the Manor House and elsewhere in the High Street, afterwards residing in Herbert Road, where his son, Dr Erichsen Page (d. 1967), subsequently lived. Dr E. Sutton Page died in 1912. Dr E. Ferdinand Page succeeded his father in various local appointments, such as public vaccination officer, medical officer to the Infirmary and police surgeon. He took up lathe work as a hobby, producing hundreds of shell cases in the First World War – and was commended by the War Office.

Several of these rather imposing Victorian villas, between Mill Lane and the Saddler's Arms, later had one-storey additions in front. Whittington's the grocers is in the distance. Winston Churchill, on a pre-Election rally after the Second World War, paused at this spot to talk to supporters.

The Grenville Institute for Men bore eminent witness to the generosity of Mrs Annie Grenville who died in 1937. One recalls it earlier as the Bivouac, or familiarly as the 'Bivvy', serving the same recreational purposes in a shop fronting on to the Victorian houses between Mill Lane and the Saddler's Arms. Mrs Grenville also built the (now Royal) British Legion Hall in Union Road, later enlarging it, as well as Sheldon Institute, and contributed largely to the Evans Convalescent Home in Widney Manor Road.

A 1970s view of Quinet House, with Tustin's butcher's shop in the distance. Grumpy William Chinn, the previous butcher, hoped it would rain on Sundays, and 'keep the motorists off the road'. He sold good meat, but did tell customers, 'if you want to be well, go to bed hungry!'

Quinet House (formerly The Limes and home of Dr E. St John Whitehouse), probably late seventeenth century, now has startling new neighbours. Unfortunately, the 'terracotta' house which also flanked Old Lode Lane is no more, but garden and clock tower on that site are pleasing, thanks to benefactor Horace Brueton.

Dr Edwin St John Whitehouse (1867–1957) of The Limes was a dear friend and counsellor to many of us, a fine sportsman, if not quite so handy with motor cars which sometimes overturned. He received an MBE for his medical work for wounded soldiers (there were 1,211 patients) at the Hermitage, Lode Lane, in the First World War and, despite advancing years, was ARP commandant of the medical section in the Second. Paul Quinet, a Belgian refugee in the First World War, came to live with him and his sister, returning to England after army service to become an eminent surgeon, saying 'he remained a father to me for the rest of his life'. Dr Whitehouse was a governor of Solihull School and of Malvern Hall Girls' School, later Solihull High School, and President of the Grenville Institute. He moved from The Limes to The Crescent. Mr Quinet and family took over The Limes.

The old Barley Mow was largely demolished in about 1900 by Showell's Brewery. A noted coaching inn, it was earlier called the Limerick Castle. John Burman suggested that a landlord may have been an old soldier who had served at the Siege of Limerick under William III. A Limerick man, Thomas Smith, was, in fact, a churchwarden in 1720.

The Barley Mow was rebuilt by Showell's in about 1900, but sustained alteration between the wars when the turret was removed – what a pity! The Solihull fire station was located here at one time, and a cattle market. The drinking fountain for horses has gone, like the weigh house in the upper picture.

Lloyds Bank, Poplar Road. Solihull's first bank (except for a savings bank) was opened in 1877 in part only of the attractive, gabled building, with accommodation for the manager above. It has lost some chimneys and the balustrade with shrubs. P.H. Sharpley, Father's solicitor, had an office adjoining; as a little boy I thought his brass plate, with 'late King and Ludlow', referred to King George V! Ludlow, of course, was a well-known Solihull name. Earlier the local gas company had premises there. I recall the James family living upstairs, and the Revd J.C. Adams, curate, and family, later of Touchwood Hall and Hampton-in-Arden, where Mr Adams was Vicar.

Still faintly remembered is the arrival of Mrs Grenville in her big green Daimler with brass lamps, chauffeur and possibly footman in attendance. She did not alight, the bank manager joining her in the car for business discussion. To the delight of watching clerks, the upholstery was sprayed, apparently with disinfectant, when he got out. Shopkeepers stood deferentially at the car door to receive orders or to proffer goods for inspection. One gathers that a daily lamb chop was sent by Hull, the butcher, save when she had a picnic, Mrs Grenville then sitting back-to-back with the chauffeur on the grass.

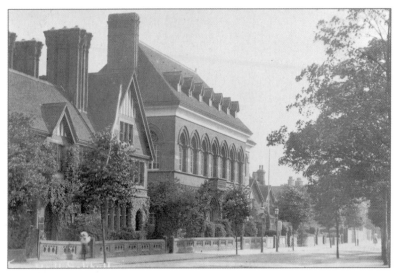

Built by the Public Hall Company in 1876, and opened with a grand ball and soirée, the Public Hall, eventually to become the Council House and just to the right of Lloyds Bank, has seen a wide variety of events – political meetings (some stormy), concerts, plays, exhibitions, bazaars, 'select' dances at 5s a head, the 1944 inauguration of Solihull Society of Arts, and the 1954 visits of HRH Princess Margaret. A ground-floor room was used as the Magistrates' Court. The annual 'Aged Women's Tea' was given by 'The Ladies of Solihull', as the invitation card said. Mother's first memory of the Public Hall was a Christmas Party given by the Misses Edwards for the 'young ladies' of the school, fires blazing at either end of the big assembly room upstairs. Bronze satin dancing slippers had been bought for her and her sister. A bossy grandmother, aghast at such 'extravagance', made their mother exchange the slippers for buttoned boots. 'We must have looked "guys",' Mother would say bitterly, years afterwards. At the time of writing, the hall is for sale after office use, and the 'new' Civic Hall has been demolished.

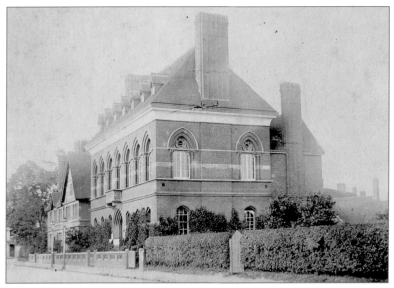

After this old view, a stage was added to the right. Council House enlargement included a much-needed lift. A police station to the right succeeded the original in New Road. This has been replaced by the one in Homer Road. Oddly, the bank building appears to have been completed before the Public Hall opened.

My sister, Laura, in the 'daffodil' dress made by Auntie 'Tot' for a school entertainment in about 1906 which could have ended in disaster. While she was dancing, paper garlands were ignited by gas footlights – yes, gas footlights! The quick-thinking girl managed to stamp out the flames before any great harm was done. The Public Hall certainly had its moments. A local 'big-wig' was chased out of the hall after making derogatory remarks about an ex-Serviceman. A rival candidate hired a hurdy-gurdy in a vain attempt to drown speeches. The old Solihull Musical Society had a particularly gifted conductor with an unfortunate habit of unduly extending the interval by dalliance in the Barley Mow. On one occasion, despite copious draughts of coffee, a substitute had to take over for the second half of *Madam Butterfly*. An audience at a lecture waited breathlessly for a speaker, who also had had too much liquid refreshment, to fall off the rather high stage. He didn't.

Curtis House, Poplar Road, was the home of Charles and Dorothy Curtis, children of the celebrated hunting-parson, the Revd Charles Curtis. Dorothy was apparently ill for many years; children thought that the prayers for her were part and parcel of the church service. Originally the front garden was larger, but the archway was subsequently rebuilt nearer the house, scene of tea parties I often attended in the Hobdays' time.

Curtis House, partially screened by additions, c. 1950. Previously, Duddy's shop occupied the old Barber Hopkins and Hobday premises at High Street – Drury Lane corner, destroyed by a Second World War bomb. Advertised performances of *Hedda Gabler* in which the author took part, as 'Tesman' (a thankless role!), were given by Solihull Society of Arts in its early days in the Council House opposite, and also a piano recital by Tom Bromley. The houses have been virtually obscured today by more building.

CHAPTER TWO

SOUTHEND, ST AUGUSTINE'S, STATION ROAD & HIGH STREET

At the end of Poplar Road, I came to High Street and Station Road, noting small pupils gathered outside Williams the cab-driver's cottage before they proceeded in 'crocodile' to Miss Cartland's establishment in The Square. High-wheeled carts were sedulously washed outside Alfred Bragg's butcher's shop, he more genial than William Chinn. More pupils would be entering Miss Crook's 'High School' at Southend, a house once belonging to Mother's cousins, the Homer brothers. Rounding the corner by St Augustine's church, I reached my own school in Herbert Road (who was Herbert, incidentally?). Miss Mary O'Gorman, niece of the founder, Canon O'Sullivan, presided here, as she did for almost forty years; sometimes, in the past, she had taught sixty children, single-handed, save for monitors. Tall, stately, and immensely respected by parents, many, like mine, non-Catholics, she wore gloves always carefully darned and spats over highly polished shoes in winter, and walked to school or Mass with measured tread from New Road lodgings. Woe betide any boy who failed to raise his cap to her in the street; my brother, Harold, didn't on one occasion, but was excused after explaining that to lift one's cap and ride a bicycle at the same time was not the simplest of accomplishments. Etiquette, indeed, was fully taught; one knew, for instance, how to accompany a lady on the pavement, though Miss O'Gorman did permit herself one curious solecism. She said drinking tea from a saucer had also been Queen Victoria's habit.

I still hear the click of that wooden 'pistol', by which we rose or sat. A black apron helped to keep chalk off her dress when she was at the blackboard, spectacles somehow reflecting any misdemeanours when so engaged. Good English and pronunciation were as important as arithmetic, but she said 'min-ute', not 'minnit'. Some children were mystified when she urged them to acquire 'a good carriage', thinking this was some sort of vehicle. Miss O'Gorman was equally puzzled when they laughed on being told that William the Conqueror's sister was wife of a tanner. She had never heard this word for a sixpence. Perhaps it wasn't used in her native Ireland?

Sometimes I went home from school via High Street, and there were Saturday shopping expeditions with Mother or Father. It was a very different street from today, houses and cottages mingling with the inns and shops. Two corn merchants lent a rural touch, the village, of course, then almost encircled by green fields. Cobblestones and blue Rowle rag stones survived until the early 1930s. There were two doctors, and at least one barber where a boy got a haircut for 3*d*. You collected accumulators which invariably 'went down' at annoying moments, and were puzzled why Mr Winfield was 'Chymist', not chemist, his white-shrouded medicine bottles, dabbed with sealing-wax, handed to you by a maid in cap and apron at a side-door out-of-hours. Small boys admired George Conibear's dexterity with the sinister-looking bacon machine. That good man would have been horrified by wire-baskets and pre-packed butter, as much as General Ludlow in chauffeured limousine at the very thought of pedestrianisation! Girls from the renowned hand laundry pushed baskets on wheels. Madame Wright, milliner, had just one item in her window, denoting exclusivity. Mrs Entwistle's was crammed with hats; we had a family legend that Mother bought the one she was wearing when she went in. The Miss Hollands sold beautiful china and glass; they surreptitiously added to my saved-up one-and-threepence for my sister's wedding present, as Mother thought.

Little pitchers have big ears, as well as eyes; overheard, the Rector's wife murmuring 'Like buying gold!' when enquiring the price of fresh salmon. (The big Rectory was already becoming a burden.) Old men drifting towards the Gardeners' Arms or Royal Oak blamed the Government for unseasonable weather, were concerned about the General Strike and issue of truncheons to hurriedly enrolled 'Specials', though nothing untoward occurred in Solihull. 'Alderbrook Road' alleged that 'Servants nowadays only want money for cheap finery'; Alderbrook's cook declared, 'I shan't stop unless I get a wireless and a comfortable chair!'

People seemed to linger more then. Long-lived John Poulter, stationer and newsagent, who'd seen Dowager Queen Adelaide driving through Oxford, and been patted on the head by William Makepeace Thackeray, could be seen talking on his doorstep to Wilfred Usher, whose detective novels are now forgotten. I don't recollect W.H. Auden, but his parents had a house in Lode Lane. Some, however, just didn't have time to linger, Mrs Martineau from Touchwood somehow managing to bow and smile to all and sundry, as she was dragged along by an impatient spaniel. Doubleday, the dentist – painful, but efficient fillings! – scurried bag in hand from railway station to surgery.

Every child visited old Mr Cohen's sweetshop (his son a nearby tailor), 'Come in, come in, I can't put it all in the window,' and, of course, dear Miss Deebank's tiny emporium next to the ironmonger's where oil-stoves glowed warmly in winter days. But there wasn't much warmth at Mrs Walter's, with her gruff 'Where's the penny?' when one went for Grandma's *Birmingham Weekly Post*, with its engaging snippets of general information, local history and a 'Toll of the Roads', already cataloguing too many motor accidents.

Who now recalls the ex-Serviceman, outside The Gables, displaying crude drawings for a few pence, or the poor woman, jug in hands blue with cold, begging children to fetch 'wine' from licensed premises where she was banned? Or the fire engine with brass helmets and galloping steeds, and Chinese lanterns in windows for the Relief of Mafeking, the last only a memory of one's elders?

Dignified Southend was the home of Mother's Homer cousins, whose ample means derived from the East Indies. George Homer (d. 1867), churchwarden and Feoffee, gave church plate and in his will – he left nearly £60,000 – some of the money for building Bentley Heath School. A crippled brother was lowered each day by windlass from his bedroom to a room below, traces of the trapdoor visible until the house was demolished in 1936. Below is the gabled rear of Southend.

The house was later the home of the Mitchell family, eventually becoming a school under Miss Burd and later Miss Crook, who was an avid antique collector. Edith Holden, author of *The Country Diary of an Edwardian Lady*, taught here. A row of shops occupies this Station Road site.

Solihull had its first Post-Reformation Roman Catholic church in 1760, built by Hugford Hassall of The Priory, Church Hill. He also gave the land and built a presbytery. Augustus Welby Northmore Pugin originally designed the new church of 1839, later to be altered and extended, not least since the Second World War. H.T. Trinder's photograph shows St Augustine of England's church in Station Road before the turret and the big window replaced lancets. The interior displays much enhancement, by the Pippet family among others.

Greatly respected by virtually all Solihull folk, Canon Michael O'Sullivan (priest from 1877 to 1892) founded St Augustine's School. 'We're going to restore the church [St Alphege],' Rector Canon Evans said to his friend. 'And I'll be very pleased to receive it!' O'Sullivan replied.

Somewhat enlarged soon after foundation, and again more recently, St Augustine's School is at present a Parish Centre. In my day it was primitive, no running hot water, no inside lavatories, no school meals, but a good school where generations (sometimes of the same family) had an excellent, if simple, education, acknowledged by parents and pupils, although a cousin asked me if I 'still went to that Roman Cartholic (*sic*) school'. The house to the right was a Pippet family residence, now demolished.

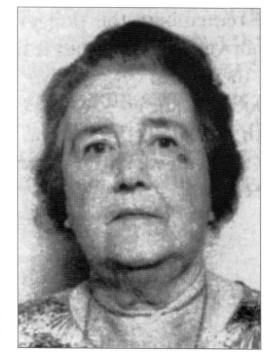

My favourite teacher was to be Miss Mary Greaney, later Mrs Beresford. (Unfortunately the photograph is very unflattering, but no other was obtainable.) My love of history is due to her, and she would even act the part of historical characters during class. Long years later I visited her in Jersey, where she lived with her sister, both widows. A little boy never dreamed that he would one day take them out to dinner in a 'swish' hotel. What an evening of reminiscence!

Opened in 1921, the Church of the Sacred Heart and St Catherine of Alexandria, Droitwich, was designed by F. Barry Peacock and was principally the gift of Walter L. Hodgkinson of Rashwood Court, who took the architect and Gabriel Pippet to Italy to study churches before building commenced. Virtually all the astonishing mosaic work was designed by Gabriel between the wars, and, despite poor health, he carried out carvings in marble, stone and wood. At his sister's wedding at St Augustine's, Solihull, he delayed the start of the ceremony in order to complete the mosaic of St Augustine over what was then the main entrance. Elphege Pippet (one of his brothers) was responsible for the carved Calvary on the Solihull churchyard wall where the old Town Hall used to be. I've heard that certain local bigots objected to it when it was first erected, even threatening damage.

Gabriel Pippet (born in 1880) with his wife, Alice (née Nicot). Artist, designer, sculptor, mosaicist, poet, friend of John Betjeman, Gabriel was a son of Joseph Aloysius Pippet, artist and designer, and Juliette (Canning). His parents had sixteen children, two dying young, four daughters becoming nuns, Dorothy, Irene, Mechtilda, Agatha. Two others, Monica and Barbara, also remained single, the former training as a nurse under Florence Nightingale. Both were noted for their ecclesiastical needlework. Ethelreda married George Victor Powell. Artistic sons, Oswald, Wilfred, Raphael and Elphege, joined the Hardman studios in Birmingham, while Michael was a freelance cartographer. Gregory was a priest. Gabriel died in Solihull Hospital, 1962, within sight of his Lode Lane birthplace, two days after Alice. She was descended from the Frenchman who introduced tobacco to France, hence nicotine.

Opposite the police station, a long, brick wall concealed the peaceful garden of Silhill House, home for many years of the Chattocks, but originally the Swan Inn. The Parade occupies the site. I remember the garden as a wilderness.

Silhill House from High Street, *c.* 1890, demolished in about 1926 and now replaced by the Parade. The cottages were demolished in about 1906. Mother saw Johnson the chimney sweep leap in delirium from an upstairs window and run up the street in his nightshirt. He died almost immediately after. Two sons were also sweeps. One had speech and hearing difficulties, but was adept at whist. The other was a fine dancer, but caused offence when, with horse and cart, he clattered noisily down the High Street during the Two Minutes' Silence.

Henry Harvey Chattock (1819–98), attorney, of Silhill House, son of Thomas Chattock. My father went to buy land from him, but was told 'we've never sold any yet, and I don't suppose we ever shall. You can have some on a lease [pronounced 'lace'] but you mustn't put any engine on it.' The family came from Castle Bromwich and played a conspicuous part in Solihull life over many years.

The Revd Thomas Nash Stephenson, Solihull curate from 1839 to 1843, figures in a hopeless romance detailed in Caroline Clive's Diary. He fell in love with Mary Jane, daughter of Thomas Chattock. They exchanged messages between Silhill House and the curate's home by means of candle signals, and opening and shutting the windows, but her father was opposed to the match, saying he would prefer his daughter 'to marry a toad'. She refused to elope. The disappointed suitor became Vicar of Shirley from 1843 to 1867, dying in 1876 when Vicar of Bromyard. Both he and Mary Jane did marry, but not each other.

High Street, *c.* 1820, probably the oldest existing picture. Lime trees – still recalled – obscure the Manor House in the distance. The Royal Oak is on the left, with near at hand the old George and Dragon, later the Magpie (hence wicker cage) and the Green Dragon, later converted to shops. The cart is said to belong to Fairfield, the carrier.

High Street, 1853. The picturesque, rugged lines of buildings would not have greatly changed since the grand, 1829 funeral of Henry Greswold(e) Lewis from Malvern Hall – four-horse carriages, ninety tenants, two by two (did they walk all the way to the interment at Yardley?) described in the very long account in the *Warwick & Warwickshire Advertiser*, 25 July, kindly extracted by Sarah Alan. Geoffrey Martineau recalled Victorian days when cattle for market or marching troops with gun-carriages could completely block the street.

Solihull High Street from the church battlements, *c.* 1930. Silhill House has been replaced by The Parade. Ye Arden cinema is to the right beyond the Royal Oak with its Showell's Brewery sign. There were still many village gardens.

One might think from old pictures that tranquillity reigned in the High Street, but there are tales that when the street was cobbled, loose stones found their way through windows. Drunks in Victorian days tied dead rats to door-knockers. Much more recently, two young bucks painted doors bright red one Christmas Eve. Omitting their own from treatment, they were soon caught by the police. An old soldier, victim of Indian sun, caused consternation in a milliner's by waving a nasty-looking sword and crying 'D'ye want anybody doing in 'ere?' After demolition, the cottages (left) were replaced by Edwardian shops, much praised by John Betjeman.

A Solihull procession, headed by local clergy, celebrates the coronation of King George V and Queen Mary in 1911. Other events included church services, 'Salute the Flag', a children's tea, athletics, fireworks and a bonfire. Archways were also erected for the (postponed) Coronation of King Edward VII and Queen Alexandra and the two Jubilees of Queen Victoria, whose Coronation was marked in Solihull and Shirley by a dinner for 800 poor people. Subscribers donated £79 for 600 lb of beef, 500 lb of plum pudding, 240 gallons of beer and ale, 200 loaves and 8 bags of potatoes. Did they get any 'greens'?

HIGH STREET,

SOLIHULL,

May 22nd, 1891.

Sir,

    I have pleasure in informing the inhabitants of Solihull and District, that I intend to commence business at the above address, on

SATURDAY NEXT, MAY 30th,

as a

General Ironmonger, Dealer in Earthenware,

AND DRY GOODS,

and hope by strict attention to business to obtain a share of your patronage.

        I am,

          Yours respectfully,

            GEORGE LINES.

NOTE.—All Goods supplied at town prices.

My parents set up two concerns simultaneously, Mother doing the accounts for both, often by lamplight, and soon with a baby on her knee. She drove into Birmingham with pony and trap, on business, sometimes getting pitched into the ditch by a frisky steed!

    Father became widely known for his work on Warwickshire and Worcestershire landed estates, including Warwick Castle, Charlecote Park, Hatton House, Weatheroak Hall, Haseley Manor, Guy's Cliffe and Packington. Iron pumps with his name are still around, if not the wooden ones for which 'pump trees' had to be bored, the groaning sound of the operation still in my ears.

Mother at the shop door, a wide variety of goods on display, including seaside spades. The picture is something of a mystery; not in the family album, it may have been the work of some itinerant photographer, and comes from Birmingham Central Library.

    Our shop was sold when we moved to Linehurst.

Oaks from small acorns grow, even if retail in Solihull, unlike wholesale and Birmingham, had its disadvantages. Out cycling one evening, Mother heard a certain 'lady' exclaim: 'Good heavens, tradespeople on bicycles; next thing we'll hear of them in the Bankruptcy Court!' The children are my sister and eldest brother, the tall boy perhaps one of Mother's brothers, the figure on the pavement unknown.

My sister, Laura Annie (1894–1980), seen here, married Victor George Pegg (1897–1982) in 1922. They kindly took me on my second visit to Llwyngwril – by train, and we got temporarily stuck in the tunnel at Wolverhampton. When we arrived I discovered that the pump outside the cottage could send draughts of icy water up your sleeve. . . . Sweeter memories are of the Welsh folk singing in the evening on the river bridge, a profusion of fuchsias, the little train at Fairbourne, picnics by mountain waterfalls. Unfortunately I called 'Mr Pugh the Garage' 'Mr Pug'! What happened to the picture postcard I duly sent to Mother? It's still missing after three-quarters of a century.

Solihull's first post office was in High Street, and must have resembled that described by Flora Thompson in *Lark Rise to Candleford*. It was in the hands of the Pearman family for over half a century until 1911. Miss Ruth Pearman is listed in 1874, under stationer, newsagent and fancy repository.

'Last delivery', 1911. The demands of the telegraph machine and several customers at the same time, to say nothing of an urgent telegram for Elmdon Hall, and the boy off duty, used to get Miss Pearman and her sister flustered. Miss Ruth is flanked by two assistants – the business had probably expanded by then – her sister refusing to come out.

The old post office before McDonald's. The 'timbering' to the right was false.

The old post office (centre) after McDonald's.

An attractive period piece, the Gardeners' Arms, on a festive occasion, date uncertain but probably Edward VII's Coronation. A partly underground pub, first The Captain Locker, now Nevada, replaces it. My uncle, William Lines, who brewed his own beer, was landlord after his father-in-law, James Bridge, who was also a nurseryman and seedsman.

A sad end to a once attractive building where my Aunt Emily annoyed customers by making them rise while she dusted their chairs!

Members of the well-known Troman family of The Elms, Lode Lane, would often be seen in the High Street. Daughters Clara and Annie (one is not sure which is which) are said to have been Siamese twins. They were noted riders to hounds, and the author recalls them at concerts – long dresses, berets, brogues and fur coats.

Mother was at school with Clara and Annie Troman who liked to play with her at Elm View. 'We can have plenty more', the girls said, when reproved for applying the soles of their shoes to the farmhouse grindstone.

A cow was usually kept at The Elms. One made a dash for liberty, followed by the sisters and brother Jack holding long poles. The unfortunate beast wedged itself in the doorway of a stationer's shop on The Parade – I've no idea how it was rescued.

One links the Troman family with bedstead manufacture in Birmingham. Unfortunately, unless aspiring to baronetage or landed gentry status, local families do not always leave many clues behind them. After the coming of the railway, well-to-do businessmen from Birmingham gradually populated Alderbrook Road, Homer Road, The Crescent and Warwick Road, often building quite 'stately' homes. Likewise, deep-rooted Solihull people do not invariably provide us with 'family trees'. We would then know more of the Braggs (still represented), Chinns, Trinders, Lindners and Leitners, the last related to other Birmingham merchants the Paytons. More, too, would be known of the Fairfields (farming, milling, music), the Martineaus of Huguenot ancestry, and their kinsfolk, the Madeleys and Harbornes; the Burbidges of Timberscombe, Hampton Lane, and neighbours such as the Feltons and Sperryns. Heatons, Jewsburys and Zairs all get lost in the mists of time, but all played, or still play, their part in Solihull affairs. Greswolds, Alstons, Birds, Gillotts, Pippets have been well researched, but one feels that albums, if often badly annotated, get discarded; diaries, letters and bills are burnt, though Hobbins correspondence and accounts have rather miraculously survived. Solihull Central Library is a mine of information, willingly given. Census returns, directories, parish registers all help us and how one wishes that, for instance, my mother had had access to a tape-recorder! She told me how William Grenville of The Grove, Lode Lane (of the firm of Grenville, Cherry Street, Birmingham) was taken for a ghost. Very deaf, he affected a long white coat for after-dinner strolls, so that motorists would avoid him. He didn't answer anybody who wished him goodnight and children were frightened of him. Mother encountered an angry crowd on the heels of the 'apparition', headed fortunately by a 'bobby', who probably saved the poor man from harm.

Dascombe, pastrycook and confectioner, usually had a splendid wedding cake on display. He catered for my sister's wedding: the Charlotte Russe, with richly flavoured cream in a 'fence' of Savoy biscuits, topped with sliced banana under a jelly glaze, was out of this world!

All that was retained of Dascombe's after demolition was the Georgian façade. Gone, too, is the old-fashioned garden where you could have ice-cream made from a secret recipe. Children asking for a 'pennyworth of stale cakes, please', didn't see much of that. Other businesses recalled include Garwood's music shop, Ledbrook's Great Western mews (with vehicles outside) and an off-licence run by the Misses Ledbrook. There were also Rowe (menswear), the Co-op, Rotherham (newsagent), Fitter (jeweller), Simpson (fishmonger), Gibbons (fish and chips), Butler, Harris, Freeman, Hardy & Willis (all boots and shoes), Fowler (tobacconist), Hans Harrison (draper), Capon (milliner), Lang (grocer) as well as Betts the billposter.

Solihull Motor Co. (Kinchins'), the 'Solihull' removed as a precaution during the Second World War. Formerly two cottages, it is now gone. The hand laundry adjoined to the left.

Carnival in High Street, 1932. Over the years Solihull has not lacked festivities, whether carnival, Coronation or Jubilee celebrations, or club days with parades of grand banners. One would have loved to have seen Victorian May Day revels when the chief of the chimney sweeps in golden crown collected cash with a big soup ladle, and 'Jack-in-the-Green' paraded in a 'cage' of evergreens. At the Peace celebrations in 1919 schoolchildren marched to Malvern Park for tea in a marquee: I lost the cup one had to bring, but still have the mug that was distributed.

The Laurels, High Street, was very probably of considerable antiquity, but given an early nineteenth-century 'dress'. Predecessor of The Gables, it was John Boulton's in 1874.

The Gables, High Street, home of Dr and Mrs Bernays for many years, may have incorporated part of The Laurels. Pulled down before the Second World War, it was replaced by Solihull's first Woolworth's and other shops.

Dr Adolphus Vaughan Bernays (died 1938), left, companion unknown, but possibly Dr Whitehouse. Very early motorist, Governor of Solihull and Malvern Hall Schools, great churchman, he is recollected in long, dark coat with astrakhan collar, spats, pale grey gloves. A little inclined to gloom, he prophesied that a friend of mine (who lived to be over sixty) 'won't see seven'.

A familiar sight in my younger days was the carriage that brought Canon and Mrs Hayter from Elmdon Rectory. The top-hatted coachman was Willard, also verger at Elmdon Church, notable for his loud 'miserable sinners' at services, as well as carefully shutting window and door at baptisms, so that one had the feeling that the infant might stifle rather than catch a chill. Intrusive squirrels and other fauna were quickly ushered out.

One day, he gave a lift to a little girl. She told me, years after, that some of her young friends made the mistake of curtseying to her as she passed! Old customs die hard. The Hayters' carriage is sometimes confused with that driven, with similar dignity, by Williams, the Solihull cabman, who plied regularly between village and railway station. One elderly lady said she liked this conveyance because 'you can see over the hedges'. Sometimes, one wishes one could do the same in modern cars.

Other cabmen are listed in directories. One Green, of the Saddlers' Arms, took the Misses Robertson (see p. 20) from Bradford House to an evening party at Berry Hall. Perhaps because of too much liquid refreshment, he omitted to leave the ladies at their home on the return journey and put the cab away at the Saddlers' Arms, with them inside. His wife, imagining there were 'goings-on', doused the sisters with a bucket of water. Green did not visit Berry Hall again.

Jasper Hall, a popular figure, would sometimes stand on his doorstep, and, observing some passing vehicle, would declare, 'That's mine!' to indicate an owner's unpaid bill as long as the street.

The fifteenth-century George and Dragon (not to be confused with the George) was destined to have many and varied uses in its long history. The photograph was taken in 1853 by R.S. Chattock, brother of Henry Harvey Chattock and a consummate artist. The Georgian building to the right became Edwin Trinder's chemist shop and eventually Shaw's coffee house, where milkmen and bakers' men enjoyed refreshments.

White tiles for a bakery, later removed, disfigured the one-time George and Dragon, but the T.P. Davis pork pies, 'in season', and with just the right amount of salt and pepper, were out of this world! Halfords succeeded Pegg's cycle shop, left. The turning into Mill Lane is visible just behind the Ford Anglia.

The melancholy end of the former George and Dragon during '60s redevelopment.

Edwin Trinder's chemist's shop at High Street – Mill Lane corner. White (1874) also lists 'breech loading cartridge manfr, and gas fitting warehouse, Church Hill'. Edwin, 'whom we profanely called "Old Trinidad",' says Prebendary Smythe in his boyhood reminiscences, 1928, once supplied 'incense' in emergency to Canon O'Sullivan. Proving explosive, it was found to be firework mixture. Like his son Hugh, Edwin has left a valuable photographic record of Solihull.

Wisteria was formerly a feature of such walls in Solihull. Here, it extended from this pretty, Jane Austenish house to Trinder's shop. It was said that (despised) excursionists from Birmingham would ask: 'How much are the grapes a pound?' An elder tree in a country lane was mistaken for 'a fine tree o'cauliflower'.

'Jimmy Crump' (actually James Hastings and carrier from Malvern Hall lodge) collected soft water from the Streetsbrook road brook, selling it at ½d a bucket. Nineteenth-century watermen also included William Lane, whose sister kept leeches in Mill Lane, and 'Donkeyman Reynolds', whom Mother remembered. In the background is the so-called lodge to the Manor House, built by Richard Griswold in 1571; the Gothic porch was destroyed many years ago.

The Manor House is late fifteenth century in origin and almost certainly Greswold built. The lower façade (now cleared of white paint) is eighteenth century, and the central door replaces the original entrance, which would have been under the small gable. The shop just visible on the left is Blizzard's and on the right there is a glimpse of Hull's butcher's shop.

Thomas Horne, a well-to-do Birmingham ironmonger, was a tenant of the Greswolde Williams family at the Manor House, dying in 1910. He liked his drinking water from a certain spring in distant Lugtrout Lane, paying heavily for it. Whether it invariably came so far is questionable. The house was often called Lime Tree House, because of the limes outside.

Dr E. Ferdinand Page, son of Dr E. Sutton Page, bought the Manor House from 'Frank' Greswolde Williams, who was disposing of his Warwickshire estates. Dr Page was a considerable sporting man, who loved hunting and shooting.

Mrs Ferdinand Page (née Richards) married at St George's, Hanover Square, in 1895. She is seen here with her sons, Erichsen, who became a doctor and Robert, a nurseryman, and daughter, Peggy (Margaret?).

'The Doctor's Car,' a reproduction from a centenary volume of the Royal Birmingham Society of Artists, by James Valentine Jelley, local artist. The car outside the Manor House is Dr Ferdinand Page's, but despite the help of the artist's son, Dr John Jelley, and many others, the original has not come to light. An Arthur Capon picture of the house is in the Manor House.

After Dr Page left for Herbert Road, the Manor House was purchased by Ansell's Brewery for conversion into licensed premises, never to be realised. The Home Guard occupied it in the Second World War. Before the end of the conflict, prominent residents urged that it should be bought for preservation and public use. A hard struggle – not without opposition – ensued, but resulted in purchase for £8,000, an extra £4,000 being raised for repairs. Much more has been spent subsequently. The house is now offices and a popular restaurant, with rooms for use by various organisations.

Solihull's picture-house, Ye Arden, later Solihull Cinema, opened in 1926. The opening ceremony was performed by Miss Queenie Thomas, an actress from British silent film days. She caused a surprise by arriving in an American car with a black chauffeur. Prior to the 'talkies', there was a live orchestra, and occasionally a vocalist, one singing 'I dreamt I dwelt in marble halls' before *The Bohemian Girl*, in which an elderly Ellen Terry played a small part. The Royal Bank of Scotland occupies the site, the frontage rebuilt in accord with the old cinema.

At first, Ye Arden had a manageress, Mrs Lord, who in evening gown welcomed patrons like a duchess at a ball. Mother and I attended on the opening night, Mrs Lord telling us there were no vacant 'ninepennies', but 'some very nice "sixpennies".' We waited for the 'ninepennies'. Father always chose the balcony, where we sat with the 'nobs,' for 1s 6d. Audiences were quick to complain if a film was 'not quite "Solihull".' The major film at the opening was *The Man on the Box*, with Syd Chaplin.

An 1853 photograph of the Royal Oak, the street completely cobbled. The house with dormers immediately to the left was replaced by Ye Arden and was one of the homes of the Tromans; it had a vinery at the rear.

The Royal Oak, now no more, has begun to lose its original Georgian character in this picture, which dates from about 1900. Films were shown in a marquee in the inn yard before the advent of Ye Arden, which was many years hence.

My parents recalled barber William Hopkins who, last century, had his premises at the High Street – Drury Lane corner. Father said that, having dealt with the hair on one side of your head, you would have to turn round before the other was tackled. Hopkins declared that he had had a certain gun 'ever since it was a pishtol', and thrilled small boys with tales of giant pike in the Malvern Hall ponds. He and a daughter played at country-house dances, trudging miles, he with her harp on his back, she with his famous violin. Mrs Hopkins, noted for her lace caps, donned wooden pattens to swill out the shop, and would have been furious to know that it was bombed in the Second World War.

The Misses Blizzard, twins, outside their greengrocers' shop by the Manor House. Kindly souls, they would fetch you a screw of parsley from the garden at the rear. A customer asked for a pennyworth, then said, 'Oh a halfpennyworth will do'; 'and we'll wait for months for the bill to be paid!' exclaimed one sister. A certain dowager telephoned Hull, the butcher nearby, for cat's meat, then cancelled the order when Pussy caught a mouse.

Late with
CHAMBERLAIN, KING & JONES, LTD.

ESTABLISHED 1883.

Cabinet Works—
Woodbridge Road,
Moseley.

HIGH STREET, SOLIHULL.
(CORNER OF DRURY LANE),

Mr Jewsbury   *April* 1912

Dr. to **LEONARD J. HOBDAY,**

HIGH-CLASS UPHOLSTERER AND CABINET MAKER,

DESIGNER AND MAKER OF FURNITURE.

Furniture
Drawing Room Suites
Dining Room Suites
Made to order or Re-covered.

Chesterfields
Lounges
Settees
Divans
Grannies
and other Luxurious Chairs.

Loose Covers
A Speciality.

Bedroom Suites
Wood Bedsteads
Bedding
Mattresses
Feather Beds
Bolsters and Pillows
Re-made.

All kinds of Blinds made
and fitted.

French Polishing in all
branches.

Description	£	s	d
Nov 17/11. To moving 2 chairs		1	0
Feb 24/12 " 18ft Pine @ 2½ft		3	9
cutting to size & planing		1	6
April 9/12 " Laying Lino		1	6
" 11/12 " " "		2	0
" 13/12 " Easying Door		1	0
" 1 Bath Room Board, Stained		1	0
" 17/12 " 1 Jacobean Bedroom Suite			
made to Order	25	0	0
" 1 Bedstead to match	6	10	0
" 1 Set of Bedstead Irons & fittings		7	6
18/12 " Removing Furniture from Mr Vapors		2	6
30/12 " Moving Bureau		1	0
May 3/12 " Easying Doors & etc		1	9
4/11 " 4 Oak Chairs in Velvet			
Hide £ 2. 5. 0 ea	9	0	0
	£41.	14.	6
credit for Plys	£	4	3
	£41.	10.	3

2½%

40 9 6

Re _____ with thanks
By _____
Leonard _____

Philip Jewsbury, Solihull banker, setting up house in George Road prior to marriage in 1912, bought furniture from L.J. Hobday's (Barber Hopkins's old shop), including a made-to-measure Jacobean bedroom suite for £25. An oak table from the Old Curiosity Shop, Broadway, was £32 17s 6d. A Birmingham antique-dealer charged £8 for an oak dresser. Elsewhere, a Wilton pile stair carpet (10 yards), £1 12s 6d, copper warming-pan 8s 6d. Times have changed!

On their honeymoon the Jewsburys learned of the *Titanic* disaster.

Miss Elcox's shop, on the right of this Victorian photograph, was taken over by Miss Annie Deebank ('Speak up, moi dear, I'm a little heard of hearing'). It was crammed with everything from toys and children's books to pencils, drawing-pins, picture postcards of the village (perhaps a trifle out of date) and coloured paper that you didn't quite know what to do with when you'd bought it.

A street scene in front of the Maltshovel, kept in 1797 by William Gibbs, Gentleman, Mayor of the Court Baron, who would have been mightily surprised to see it as first the Snooty Fox, and now Rosie O'Brien's Pump House and nightclub. Beside the Masons' Arms, by the left-hand tree, was the White Cat, now the Fat Cat, which was opened between the wars by a Mr and Mrs Rea, the latter the author of a cookery book. In the distance, left, is a glimpse of Faherty's old shop, where cooked tripe, pigs' trotters and chitterlings were sold. This is probably a 1930s picture.

A delightful 'Adam' firegrate from the demolished White Swan in Knowle, photographed in a flat in Solihull High Street.

Christmas 1908, outside the Masons' Arms, with landlord Joseph Walker, Mrs Walker and son – by the barrel. Beef from the Cattle Show at Bingley Hall, Birmingham, a great annual event, is on display.

CHAPTER THREE

THE SQUARE

Munching a bun from Faherty's, I passed through The Square, Coronation lamp soon to be replaced by war memorial. One day, I'll realise that many 'ghosts' haunt this spot: the de Odingsells who gave us so much of the glorious church; benevolent Rector, John Howman, last Abbot of Westminster, who died for his faith in Wisbech Castle; Sir George Throckmorton, his patron and lord of the manor, riding over from Coughton Court; Cavaliers and Roundheads – probably Charles I himself – clattering through, long before that colourfully uniformed troop raised to assist the Militia and defy Napoleon. The Revd Andrew Archer pauses to tell a parishioner of that dinner given by Mistress Holbech of Bentley Heath – Pig Disguised, Peachick, Snow, Whole Preserved Lemons – though he won't have too much time, expiring soon afterwards! A foolhardy youth climbs a spire soon to fall in a March gale, detailed so well by Edward Bratt from his draper's shop in the High Street. Wealthy Benjamin Palmer from Olton End, over 6 ft, but with the legs of a small child trots into church ahead of his many servants, crossing the place where Sarah Court and Sarah Edwards are whipped for stealing cabbage. Here, perhaps, the village constable hands that reluctant shilling to the intinerant 'man and great bawling woman' for food and drink. Grand obsequies – mutes and sable plumes – contrast with Widow Grant's funeral which costs the parish nearly 5s, including ale for the mourners. School dancing lessons (no conversation between the sexes permitted) are in the Town Hall where magistrates preside. Hounds meet, Curfew rings out (alas, no longer as I write). Carriages – 'the horses' heads turned towards Malvern Hall' as per instruction – await a congregation at a sacred concert. Swingboats bruise churchyard limes at the fair. An elderly Victorian bride shrieks 'fools, fools!' as villagers cheer and throw rice, Mother remembers. At school lunchtime, I shall witness a wedding when, rumour has it, a big-wig's daughter will be shot by a jilted admirer. Nothing happens. Mrs Lowe, a Victorian doctor's wife, is late for service (she always is) but not the Howard Heatons, 'Solihull's best-dressed couple,' top hat, morning-coat et al, or neat, but too conspicuous workhouse children, briskly escorted.

Joseph Pippet the artist, and son of the agent to the Coughton estate, lived in this house, I am told, removing to Lode Lane when his family grew. I remember it as a dental surgery, with Harrison Thompson, undertaker, next. The war memorial has now been moved nearer to the church.

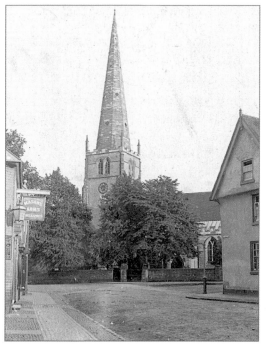

St Alphege's church is Solihull's architectural glory, including a wonderful thirteenth-century chancel, crypt and chantry chapel. The collapse of the ancient spire in 1757 greatly damaged the church. Clapham Holbech climbed the old one either by the angle crockets or steeplejacks' ladders. Thrashed by his churchwarden father as a consequence, he ran away and was drowned abroad in 1737. (He is called 'The Steeple Flyer' in the family tree.) The new spire has also been troublesome and has been partly rebuilt. Eliza Wise from Knowle made a climb by ladders in the last century and handed a glass of port to a workman at the top. 'Hughie' Trinder, by repute, tried an ascent but got his photographic equipment entangled in a ladder, and was rescued with difficulty.

This picture shows The Square without the war memorial.

John Burman thought this intriguing row – ancient timbers, not so ancient brickwork, blocked doorways within, tales of hauntings – might have been the Baynton family mansion. Now offices, threatened demolition was avoided after the Second World War, and rendering removed. After serving as houses, then an extension to Powell's School nearby, it was again divided and also served as a school run by the Misses Mary and Sarah Ann Cattell – the 'Red Cow' and the 'Brown Cow' respectively, as described by irreverent youngsters. This was attended by the future Prebendary Smythe, Rector's son, utterly terrified on his first morning by an older brother's teasing 'information' that the good ladies kept a steam thrashing-machine! Their assistant, Miss Charlotte Brown, is still just remembered with her Pomeranian dog.

A Victorian picture of performing bears in The Square. This would be at one of the fairs often much disliked by local folk, as they brought in undesirables from 'Brummagem'. Mother and her sister had an unfortunate ride on one of the roundabouts; both were ill in consequence, Auntie blaming Mother for wanting the ride, but Mother said that it was Auntie who had wanted it. Oral history can mislead.

The Town Hall and successor to an earlier hall, or halls and other buildings, including houses, alongside the church, was built in 1779 and demolished (for £12) in 1880. Chains from cells beneath are in the church. The fire-engine was housed here, as well as the stocks, the latter disappearing one 5 November.

Designed by W.H. Bidlake, the Birmingham architect, Solihull's war memorial was unveiled on 21 June 1921 by the Earl of Craven, Lord-Lieutenant of Warwickshire. Owner of the great Coombe Abbey estate, near Coventry, he fell to his death from a yacht in the Solent, on 10 July following.

Miss Kathleen Cartland, Dame Barbara Cartland's cousin, with assistant and pupils at Ruckleigh School, 1924. 'Carty', as she was invariably known, opened her school – next to The Priory – in 1909. It was eventually transferred to one of the large Victorian houses in Warwick Road, between Mill Lane and Poplar Road, afterwards to the corner of Warwick Road and Mirfield Road, then to Lode Lane where it flourishes today. A child's writing slate and an original desk are preserved by the present principal, together with photographs of various periods.

Hugford Hassall of The Priory (founder, as we have seen, of Solihull's first Post-Reformation Roman Catholic church) used to entertain Joseph Weston, parish church organist, whilst Rector Curtis was preaching. Unfortunately Weston was a poor timekeeper, and often too late for the concluding hymn, so he was eventually dismissed. Poet and great dandy, with the curious habit of exchanging his clothes with passing mendicants, he was buried in Solihull churchyard after a period in Henley-in-Arden asylum.

The old Priory at the top of Church Hill was never a priory in the strictly religious sense, but may have sheltered dispossessed Benedictine nuns from Henwood Priory following the Dissolution. After housing Powell's School it was the home of the Paytons, a merchant family. It was demolished in 1889, when it was said to be very dilapidated. The photograph shows a 'cock horse' which would assist vehicles up the steep hill.

When the one-time Powell's School gave way to a new house in 1889, this summerhouse in the old garden was retained. It was the usual sleeping place of two Spanish pupils who preferred the spiders to the alleged ghost of a headmaster who had hanged himself. Caroline Clive's Diary reveals that, in 1838, headmaster John Powell took his own life by poison. This pretty building has been demolished.

The Priory, as the celebrated Powell's School. This was started elsewhere by John Powell and continued by a nephew, John Powell junior; both were ushers at the Grammar School. Fights were frequent between Grammar School boys ('Tadpoles'), and Powell boys ('Bull-dogs'). The old drawing shows shopkeeper 'Mother' Aston selling sweets to pupils.

Members of the Matthews family of The Priory, Solihull, earlier of Olton, and for a time living in Rome. Mischievous-looking George, seated centre, hoped to become a monk, but health did not permit. I think we have sister 'Winnie' on the left, and 'May' on the right. I am not so sure about the others. The family had a cook who served so long that eventually the sisters gave her breakfast in bed.

Sir George Throckmorton, lord of the manor of Solihull from 1528 to 1554, and patron of the living, lived at Coughton Court, near Alcester, building the magnificent gatehouse there. By his wife, Anne Vaux, he had eight sons and eleven daughters. The manor was sold of necessity by his grandson, unfortunate Thomas, who paid very heavy fines as a recusant. The present lord of the manor is Mr David Couchman.

Roast fox for dinner. 'If you catch him, I'll eat him!' said Rector Curtis, after a particularly hard run, to his huntsman, Joe Pitchford. Reynard was eventually caught, but whether actually consumed is doubtful. Perhaps it proved as uneatable as Oscar Wilde suggests.

   Rector of Solihull from 1789 until his demise in 1829, and also of St Martin's, Birmingham, from 1781 to 1829, Charles Curtis was brother of Sir William Curtis, Lord Mayor of London in 1798. In Nonconformist view (somewhat jaundiced?) he was more addicted to the sports of the field than parishioners' spiritual welfare. Pemberton, picturing the jovial cleric often riding over to St Martin's to assist Dr Croft, his Perpetual Curate there, is far more charitable. In Caroline Clive's Diary, his successor writes of Curtis's second wife, Sarah (Wilkieson) who lived until 1852: 'Mrs Curtis wears well with the help of rouge and a black wig and white powder. She does not wash.'

Rector Curtis's charming home probably dated from before Elizabethan times, and was demolished by his successor, the Revd Archer Clive, something that would provoke an outcry today! A fragment, perhaps from an even older house, survives near the path into the churchyard.

The Revd Archer Clive, Rector from 1829 to 1847, grandson of his patron, second and last Lord Archer of Umberslade, was part-author of Caroline Clive's Diary. This has been edited by Lady Mary Clive, whose husband, Major G.D. Clive, killed in the Second World War, was his great-grandson, the major's father being a victim of the First World War. Although self-deprecating in this respect, he ran the parish with ability, even if one relative thought him 'high-handed'. He and his wife lived in state at the new Rectory, handsomely entertaining friends and villagers, ninety present at a servants' ball, visitors arriving at 7 p.m. and departing at 6 next morning.

Mrs Archer Clive (born Caroline Meysey Wigley in 1801 – see also p. 116), poet, novelist and diarist, was an heiress and owner of Olton Hall. Lame through infantile paralysis, she nevertheless led an active life, riding and travelling for many years. After their marriage in 1840, the couple were greeted on arrival in Solihull by triumphal archways and addresses. In 1873 life in retirement on their Whitfield (Herefordshire) estate was wrecked when she died in a fire.

Greatly loved Patrick Murray Smythe, Rector from 1847 to 1872, previously curate of Tanworth. There is a charming description of him among the roses and hovering butterflies of the Rectory garden by his son, Prebendary Smythe of St Ninian's, Perth, in a rare fête souvenir of 1928. Poor man, he had only one eye, a disability shared with his curate, the Revd Samuel Wright, and verger, Frederick Chinn.

The Revd Charles Evans, Rector from 1872 to 1894, was head of King Edward's School, New Street, Birmingham, where he had been a pupil under Dr Prince Lee, whose daughter he married. He built and lived at The Hermitage in Lode Lane before moving to the Rectory, and had an observatory with revolving roof there. He was a keen local historian, and much church restoration took place during his time.

The Revd Thomas Beedle Harvey Brooks succeeded Canon Evans, having been previously incumbent of St Stephen's, Battersea, and St Stephen's, Paddington. One recalls what even then seemed archaic clerical garb. On retirement in 1928 he and his wife went to live in an Oxfordshire cottage, a contrast to the rectory he had found somewhat difficult to maintain; in fact, before the First World War he would retire to a modest New Road house during the summer, letting the Clive 'mansion'.

Rector Clive's Solihull rectory, built with bricks made at the foot of Church Hill. The house had a magnificent library and panelling from Henwood Hall, the latter preserved in the present smaller house. A butler and footman were employed, as well as a personal maid for Mrs Clive, among other domestics. Below the formal garden was an avenue where the friendly societies would meet with their processional banners.

Two Solihull rectories at one time, 1930s. The photograph was taken from the church battlements by 'Cliff' Joiner, the camera setting by 'Hughie' Trinder (who could no longer climb the steps). The Clives' nineteenth-century rectory is the older building at the rear.

James Holliday, verger from 1861, last to hold the additional (civil) office of parish beadle in Solihull, died in 1902 on his way to church. He often acted as a part-time fireman, being called from a service to a fire at Powell's Farm (my great-uncle's) on one occasion, as well as master of ceremonies at local dances, his wife in the cloakroom. A search for his uniform, years ago, for an exhibition, revealed that he was buried in it.

A group by the south chancel door, St Alphege's church, *c.* 1930. Seated is the Revd C.O.R. Wormald (formerly Wormell), rector from 1928 to 1935, and formerly RAF chaplain and curate to the Revd T.B. Harvey Brooks, whose daughter he married. He was subsequently Vicar of Oakham, Rutland. Standing from left to right: H.T. Trinder, assistant verger and village photographer, John Bass, verger, and organist Courtenay Woods, who introduced fine music to numerous local schoolchildren by special recitals. He greatly enjoyed tea parties and was much loved. Appointed in 1886, he died in retirement in 1944.

A photograph, by H.T. Trinder, 1911, when St Alphege's church weathervane was brought down for regilding by Charles May of Bragg Bros, builder. Standing, left to right: John Bass, verger; Charles Bragg snr, builder; a workman, Arthur Stowe; a workman, Tom Tarplee, and Roland Bragg. Seated: Robert Bragg; a workman. Much church work was proceeding at this time. The vane was probably purchased in 1775, about the time the spire was rebuilt after the serious fall of 1757. The old weathercock was sold for 4s 6d. The Braggs have held prominent positions in local business and church life over the years. Charles Bragg snr was captain of the volunteer fire brigade.

The George Hotel, now Jarvis International, was earlier the Bell then the Nag's Head. Much frequented by local gentry, it was a coaching inn, but more coaches called at the Barley Mow. This is an early picture. Curiously, recent restoration has deprived the building of two gables and the pretty Georgian doorway was lost to a poorer entrance.

The George lost its prized wisteria through a leaking gaspipe, but this was survived by one in Park Road. The cottages there have now been destroyed. In this photograph Mrs Hillman, the landlady, is probably at the door. The coaching party is possibly a local one but brakes came out from Birmingham at weekends.

Fletcher Henry, plumber, Warwick road
Galloway Frederick, tailor, High street
George first-class family & commercial hotel (Joseph Hill-
    man, proprietor), wine, spirit & cigar merchant, re-
    freshment contractor & first-class bowling green &
    cricket grounds; large & commodious commercial,
    club & smoking rooms, billiards, poole & pyramids;
    balls, banquets & wedding breakfasts catered for in
    first-class style; masonic lodge held here the first Wed-
    nesday in each month, High street
George & Wilsdon, carriage builders, New road

'Joe' Hillman's establishment seems from this entry in Kelly's *Directory* of 1908 to have been a worthy forerunner of the present much enlarged and restored Jarvis International Hotel. 'Joe' would have been pleased to see the George signboards retained as a concession to local sentiment, even if the sight of electric fire and fire-irons would have astonished him.

    A neighbour of ours, Charles Sinclair, wrote that in 1905, when he first came to Solihull, he encountered 'Joe' Hillman. He said that 'Joe' was 'quite a versatile Shakespearian scholar, one of his many visitors . . . Barry Sullivan, the great tragedian'. Hillman told him 'they would have a bottle of wine together, and a long chat, after a game of bowls on the historical bowling-green'. 'Joe' was followed after his death by Mrs Hillman as landlady.

Mrs Stewart (formerly Mrs Hugh Taylor), hostess of the George 1828–1868, aunt of Hugh Taylor Trinder, village photographer. She would know the decline of coaching days and the coming of the railway to Solihull in 1852. Hugh Taylor helped to establish a racecourse on the Olton side of Solihull.

    Mrs Stewart's nephew and niece, Hugh and Polly Trinder, treasured relics of the George in their house in The Square, including a 'yard of ale' glass, but these seem to have been thrown away as 'junk' when their possessions were dispersed. Fortunately, however, photographic slides were acquired by my old friend, the late David Jewsbury, and photographs are in the Joiner Collection in Solihull Library. Some precious negatives were found doing duty in cold-frames on an allotment, and others in a lamp over the parish church gate!

Looking from the church battlements over the George and its famous bowling-green, 1911. Some houses have been built in George Road; others appear in course of construction. All have gone.

Four-bedroomed villas were built at the Drury Lane end of George Road in about 1911, as well as smaller homes opposite. Development then waited until after the First World War, when three-bedroomed houses, also semi-detached and with no brick garages, filled most of the vacant space, and were described in estate agent's jargon as having 'two reception-rooms', one really dining-room-cum-kitchen, the other not big enough to swing the proverbial cat in. A single house was called 'The Oddity'.

In 1890 Linden House, just left of the George, was sold by the Governors of Solihull United Charities to 'Joe' Hillman for £800. It had been occupied by a Dr Palmer who, answering a call to a patient in the night, fell headlong from the bedroom window. His wife, seeing his predicament, rushed downstairs, the door slammed behind her, and both were left in the chill air and their night attire. The pavement was hard; one hopes the good doctor escaped injury. Earlier, the Misses Bryett and others had one of the many young ladies' schools there.

The work of Solihull United Charities is explained in *Solihull and its School*, by John Burman, a former Governor. This also has an account of the preceding Feoffees going back to about 1560, when Thomas Dabridgecourt of Longdon Hall presided over a body of trustees for various benefactions and accompanying properties. The Feoffees were also, in Pemberton's words, 'a kind of local Parliament', controlling the Grammar School, Town Hall, fire engine and public weighing-machine. They helped to finance the parish church; the accounts over the years refer to such items as 'warming the church in winter' and repairs to the spire. Scattered properties included a one-time neighbour of Linden House. This was Holywell House (near the site of St Alphege Well), demolished in 1800 for an extension to the churchyard. The worthy members of the little Parliament were drawn from gentry, surgeons and yeomen to draper, carpenter, tanner, innkeeper and others. Some served for long periods; builder Thomas Harborne of High Street for fifty years (he was also churchwarden for a like period) but exceeded by surgeon John Short, whose total was fifty-seven! The Feoffees continued in office until 1879, being succeeded by the Governors of the United Charities. One rather wishes the old name could have been retained.

The old Grammar School of sixteenth-century foundation, and attended by the poets William Shenstone and Richard Jago, is a mixture of styles and dates. Dr Samuel Johnson was refused the headmastership. It was known when in private occupation as Malvern House, used as a preparatory school for its successor, then as a hotel and was derelict before rescue. A little girl, leaning from a window in 1757, cried 'Look nurse, the church spire's falling down!' She was rebuked for a lie, but it was true.

The old Grammar School was not lost but survives on the Park Road – New Road corner. Threatened, New Road has undergone a considerable amount of refurbishment.

Despite past threats, New Road retains much Victorian dignity. The original Solihull police station is said to have been its first building. White's directory (1874) mentions Inspector Jesse Welch and eight constables after its enlargement. remember the Aldingtons (see p. 28) when it was a private house, cells intact, and conversion into shops meant a sub-post office was here for a time. The homes of Herraty, Banks, Harmer, Deebank, Fairfield (pianos on sale), Rigg, Godson Daffern, Jelley (see p. 68) all come to mind. Miss Capner of Golden Lion vintage had witch-like shoes, sported both walking stick and 'husband-beater' umbrella, and said 'my complaint is Anno Domini'. The Misses Burman came from a very old Warwickshire family which has produced a Member of Parliament, knighthoods, Lord Mayors for Birmingham Mayors of Stratford-upon-Avon, neighbours for Anne Hathaway, grand old farmers and hunting-men, magistrates and historians. The ladies kept a tiny school – shades of Joyce Grenfell! – flourishing a feather duster when a small pupil was naughty. Miss Palmer had a 'select' guest house and the Miss Goodalls had servant problems. The Misses Cook were daughters of Daniel Cook, landlord of the High Street's Maltshovel. Miss Ruth Pearman, the old postmistress, owned a lot of rather dusty Victoriana. The cantankerous Miss Shuttleworths bullied a bachelor brother: 'I give 'em twenty-five shillings a week and all the vegetables and then they throw the kidney beans at me!'

CHAPTER FOUR

WALKS WITH FATHER

One dreams of green fields once encircling Solihull, happily traversed with Father in his most reminiscent mood. Not all have vanished, but from Church Hill and the glebe meadows we could take an almost unbuilt Widney Manor Road; this led past the Evans Convalescent Home (for children needing fresh country air) and timbered Whitley Hall, this last mercifully still surviving, like contrasting Lovelace Hill, General Ludlow's old home, said to have been built in South African style. Widney Manor station, a latecomer to the line, detained us, for I was already fond of trains, though comparatively few stopped there; one that did was to put Queen Victoria to bed on her last journey to Balmoral. Thence ivied Hillfield Hall, where the Boddingtons lived, no forest of homes or complex of roads around it. Fowgay Hall was in a very different Dingle Lane. In Blossomfield I would be reminded that Great Uncle Powell at Homer House would make his nephew clean boots, pronounce them not sufficiently polished, then approving without a single further touch. The Acorns, which had been Blossomfield Farm and had links with Solihull Methodism, was to become White Falcon Lodge and gained peacocks on the lawn, eyeing themselves in a mirror. The White House, Sir Robert Bird's, seemed, like its garden, to grow bigger with the years, and Tudor Grange had the fine bronze horse and groom, now in Malvern Park. Near Regency Sutton Lodge was Hewitt's famous nursery – Gertrude Jekyll made a garden there – now replaced by Dorchester Road. The old railway station – more trains to watch – was a little nearer to Birmingham than the present one. In Station Road, Arden Grange, close to the Methodist church-cum-school, was home to the whip-making Zairs, cedars in spacious grounds now built over. Fernleigh was a reminder that nurseryman Thomas Hewitt had presented Mother, as a girl, with the rarity of a tomato from his own conservatory, only to see it thrown away in utter disgust, as 'the most horrible thing' she had ever tasted! Then Sutton Grange (not to be confused with Sutton Lodge) and the somewhat retiring Northmede, once artist Richard Chattock's home, faced other Victorian houses which still remain; these became St Martin's School for a time.

Yew Tree Lane, by Barnett's Cottage, which had roses round the door and a draw-well in the garden, meant we took the utterly rural way past our own farmland, high banks that could be choked to the brim with winter snow. There were the nurseries where one crossed a field, which might be sheer gold with buttercups, to buy cucumbers from solemn Mr Robertson, solicitor-turned-nurseryman, often to be found in one of the deliciously humid greenhouses, a sixpenny cucumber specially cut for you – and there were plenty of tomatoes! Marsh Lane had the main Berry Hall gates and long drive, flush with rhododendrons, and one had an invariable reminder that Colwall Lodge, hard by, had once been the Marsh Tavern. Malvern Park when first we went that way had a ruined bath-house, with blue and gold plasterwork before Blytheway was made – hardy gentry formerly immersing themselves in an icy stream. So, by Sandalls Bridge and the Blythe, a glimpse of the 'Barn à la Paestum', whose history I didn't then know, and an about turn for the park, to cross the grand avenue, now Brueton Avenue, for that view of classic mansion and its lovely curving porch.

On another day, a Hampton Lane clapgate yielded gabled Marsh Farm again, beyond a short avenue intended for a road waiting and waiting to be made. Fields to Ravenshow had a cricket-ground, perhaps with white-clad players, and the 'pop-pop' of an engine which helped to supply Victorian Berry Hall with electricity, as a miniature gasworks had earlier provided illumination. By Berry Old Hall, haunted, romantic, Father would point out the special little gates for gamekeepers. The wooden bridge, over the Blythe, delight of artists, led to medieval Ravenshaw Hall, and the ugly farm buildings of Cow Hayes. In Barston Lane folk spoke of hearing nightingales: Henwood Lane had Bogay Hall – a name, I believe, now changed – and the watermill with its dovecotes before the Isolation Hospital and Catherine-de-Barnes. Lugtrout Lane led us to our own farmland again, no Damson Parkways but, still there, the pretty, slightly church-like house where Great Uncle Abraham spent his last years. Our meadow had watercress to pick from a stream. You won't find any now!

Cornyx Lane took us to Wharf Lane, the Anchor, by the gasworks and canal. Or we could go on to a scarcely traffic-ridden Lode Lane for Olton Mill and its pool, and Olton Hall. Or by Olton Golf Links to Dove House Farm, thence by Warwick Road – Suffragettes had burnt a house here but not the Georgian one (now long vanished), where its owner would once walk to Solihull station followed by a manservant carrying a clean pair of boots for his master's journey into Birmingham. . . . World's End was a reminder of a vanished inn. Clothed in later brick, Broad Oaks Farm outwardly betrayed little sign of ancient Greswold occupation, though broad acres were a reminder of a one-time Solihull race-course and Seven Star Cottages of another hostelry. Alternately we might take Broad Oaks Road for a glimpse of Silhill Hall (saddening thought today!) and then back to Linehurst.

The old glebe meadows, a lunch-time resort from school in my day, from church battlements, looking towards the railway line. They were sacrificed to housing development before the Second World War, including a fine avenue leading from the rectory garden.

The corner of Church Hill Road and Whitefields Road, postmark 1906. The latter was once Garretts Green Lane, not to be confused with a lane of the same name beyond the Coventry road. Prior to William Fairfield's death in 1947, the Fairfields lived for many years at Garretts Green Farm, on the site of a moated home of the Hawe or Hawes family, afterwards of Hillfield Hall. In 1474 the name is 'Gerards', presumably denoting an owner; 1476 'Gearards'; 1478 'Garratys'; 1481 'Gearardes'.

Sixteenth-century Whitley Hall – long known as Malvern Park Farm, its land once embracing the deer-park of Malvern Hall – was sketched by John Constable on one of his visits to Solihull, but no one seems to know where the picture is.

Hillfield Hall, burnt in 1867 and restored later in the nineteenth century, is now a well-known restaurant. The initials of William and Ursula Hawes, its builders, the date 1576 and motto *Hic Hospites, in Caeli Cives*, originally appeared on the left-hand turret, but, together with the entrance doorway, have been transferred to that on the right. The Feildings were later owners of this striking brick house, including 'Beau' Feilding, a frequenter of Charles II's court. He bigamously married the equally notorious Barbara Castlemaine, Duchess of Cleveland, but had sold Hillfield just before. The Greswolds of Malvern Hall were subsequent owners. A 400th anniversary dinner in 1976 was attended by Gordon Hawes (a descendant of William and Ursula), who flew specially from America, and two American Griswolds.

Tudor Grange was built 'in Elizabethan style', to designs by T.H. Mansell, in about 1887 for Alfred Lovekin, 'regardless of expense' as a 1900 sale brochure has it. When the future Sir Alfred Bird bought the property from Lovekin, Blossomfield Road ran nearer to the mansion. He converted part of the old road into a private drive. A new stretch was made at his own cost, but this aroused the fury of a local resident who persisted in using the original route on his way to Solihull station, crying 'The King's Highway, the King's Highway!' at the top of his voice.

A portrait of Sir Alfred Frederic Bird, Bt (son of the inventor of the famous custard powder), by John Seymour Lucas. Sir Alfred was born in 1849 and accidentally killed in a London accident in 1922. Conservative MP for West Wolverhampton from 1910, he made a notable collection of statuary, and enlarged house and grounds. Tudor Grange is now part of Solihull College of Technology.

Some idea of the grandeur of Tudor Grange ('Custard Hall') in private ownership can be gauged by a programme issued to West Wolverhampton constituents for a 1913 garden party. The large party, brought by special train, inspected 'terraces, conservatories, ferneries, hot-houses and ornamental shrubberies, lake with waterfowl, Italian garden and many interesting old vases, seats, ornaments and curios', as well as the figurehead of an old warship, the *Queen Anne*. Lavish entertainment and repast were also laid on, as well as a glimpse of the interior of the house.

Elaborate woodwork (some, if not all, by the celebrated Warwick woodcarvers, Plucknett) and moulded ceilings are features of Tudor Grange, which is well looked after by its present occupants. The façade also retains much external statuary.

The arrival at Malvern Park in 1953 of the rearing horse and groom, presented to Solihull by Captain Oliver Bird MC, JP, son of Sir Alfred Bird, Bt. The statue was modelled by Sir Joseph Edgar Boehm (1834–90), Sculptor-in-Ordinary to Queen Victoria.

A very similar horse and groom by Boehm for the first Duke of Westminster. The model for this horse was an English thoroughbred called 'Citadel' and bred by Lord Derby. (By kind permission of His Grace the Duke of Westminster OBE, TD, DL.)

Lady (Robert) Bird in the grounds of The White House. Once described as 'a darling with a temperament', she was keen gardener, amateur artist and skilled needlewoman, as well as a pianist of distinction, though I never heard of a public performance. Sir Robert succeeded his father as MP for West Wolverhampton.

Solihull station, 1864; it was first opened in 1852. The well-remembered bridge came later. In 1922 my sister and I waited to see Princess Mary's honeymoon train pass by. That was all we did see; I think we were expecting to see the happy couple leaning out of a window, perhaps in wedding attire! After the theatre we loved to come home from Birmingham on the last train. The station was then slightly nearer to Olton, whose station came later. A line from Hampton-in-Arden to Catherine-de-Barnes, Salter Street and Redditch was proposed in 1843 but came to nothing.

Sutton Grange, Station Road (not to be confused with Sutton Lodge), was built for Dr E. Sutton Page, father of Dr Ferdinand Page. The architect was F.B. Endall, who also designed the author's Beechnut Lane home. Sutton Grange is now replaced by part of The Parade; Uptons, Wrights and Wards were subsequent owners.

Northmede, or Northmede Cottage, was built for Richard S. Chattock, brother of Henry Harvey Chattock of Silhill House, nearby. A solicitor like his brother, he was also a consummate artist and photographer. The house stood back from Station Road, eventually becoming a nursing home (Northmead).

My father bought Yew Tree Farm, Yew Tree Lane, from eccentric 'Frank' Greswolde Williams at about the time of the First World War. A former possession of Henry Greswold(e) Lewis of Malvern Hall (see the 'HGL' on the wall), the farmhouse, of seventeenth-century origin, was unfortunately demolished in about 1937, and much adjoining land was built on after the Second World War. My sister lived in the house for a short while, but it was normally occupied by tenants or farm workers.

Yew Tree Lane has been partly re-aligned. High banks once held driven snow. It was good to sit on a certain stile with a view of distant Yardley Church steeple, if unlike the boy in the story, not sitting there eating fat bacon all day! A whirlwind on 24 October 1923 blew down trees. My farmer brother, Frederick (1902–92), from a vantage-point nearby saw this and 'the air full of birds'. At school one knew nothing of this storm, but mothers anxiously awaited children at the gates afterwards.

Henry Greswold(e) Lewis was obviously fond of his initials. They appeared on Yew Tree Farm, and still on the fine gates of his Solihull mansion, and are also in plaster on a ceiling at Radford Hall, Radford Semele, near Leamington Spa, which also belonged to him. Others on a chimney in Radford village have gone. Radford also has a Lewis Road and The Greswoldes among its road names.

The Greswolds were of ancient Warwickshire and Worcestershire stock (the name, of course, was variously spelt) who ranged from the humble to wealthy landed gentry. The many American Griswolds are especially welcomed.

Henry Greswold(e) Lewis (1754–1829) – son of Welsh landowner, David Lewis, and Mary Greswold, heiress of Malvern Hall, Solihull – after the usual 'polite education', made the Grand Tour. He enjoyed himself in the company of John Soane, an architectural student destined to play a conspicuous part in alterations and additions to the mansion his friend had inherited from 1783 onwards. Neither was an easy character, Rupert Gunnis calling the eventual Sir John Soane (Surveyor of the Bank of England) 'of difficult temperament, austere, touchy and neurotic'. Henry has been described as 'a combination of sensitiveness and pomposity', eccentric even, who made excessive demands on John Constable, who produced several portraits of him that are now scattered like the artist's other Solihull and other Warwickshire landscapes.

Greswold(e) Lewis ('Greswold' was actually a baptismal name, that tiresome 'e' adopted later and not invariably used even then) was fortunate in material wealth but not in love. His marriage to Charlotte Bridgeman, Lord Bradford's daughter, was a disaster. He writes affectionately of her but avows having 'married not only herself but her family and all their follies as well'; an unstable mother introducing laudanum to her daughter, ruining her already precarious health, and Lord Bradford signing away her inheritance. The couple parted, were reconciled, and Charlotte died in 1802, childless and prematurely aged.

Strangely, despite Henry's sweeping condemnation of Charlotte's family, the celebrated 'Ladies of Llangollen' (see *The Ladies of Llangollen*, by Elizabeth Mavor, Michael Joseph, 1971) spoke highly of the fine moral tone of host, hostess and offspring when they visited Weston Park, the Bradfords' seat in Staffordshire, and they were not alone in recording praise. Odd, too, that Henry should send his portrait to a brother-in-law! He never remarried, in loneliness doting on a ward, Mary Freer, probably an illegitimate relation of David Lewis, aforesaid. Estates – Malvern Hall, a park with deer from nearby Aston Hall, and a French chef to cook the venison – passed to a kinsman of old Greswold descent, Edmund Meysey-Wigley, who had to change his surname to Greswolde. Edmund soon died on military service in Ireland, and was succeeded by an uncle who also became 'Greswolde'.

Henry's ward, Mary Freer, later Mrs
Ffrance, by John Constable, 1809. It is
now in the Mellon Collection, New
Haven, Connecticut, which also has
one of Constable's views of the
entrance-front of Malvern Hall. Mary
was well provided for in her guardian's
will.

Elizabeth (Lewis) Lady Croft, also by
Constable. She made as unfortunate a
marriage to Sir Herbert Croft, Bt, as
that of her brother Henry's to
Charlotte Bridgeman. Although in
Holy Orders, and the author of
'several entertaining and useful works,
among them the well-known *Love and
Madness*,' says Burke, Sir Herbert was
anything but a model clergyman, and
gave his wife (his third) much
unhappiness. This portrait was recently
sold.

Lady Croft's two sisters married two
brothers, who became Earls of Dysart
in turn.

Solihull rector, Henry Greswold (who died in 1700 and came from his family home in Greet in Yardley parish) bought the Malvern estate adjacent to his rectory. His son Humphrey built Malvern Hall, later extended by Greswold(e) Lewis, and through the Wigleys (Greswoldes) and the Williams family of Pitmaston, Worcester, it descended to 'Frank' Greswolde Williams who sold it in 1896.

Edmund Greswolde's brother, the Revd Charles Meysey Wigley, suffered a fatal fall downstairs after a lively evening with friends in 1830. This staircase remains, but there were several others prior to the demolition work.

The balustrade of the Malvern Hall main staircase is to John Soane's design. A William and Mary balustrade, which was a feature of the old house, is now at Shakespeare Hall, Rowington.

After David Troman bought Malvern Hall, he demolished the top central storey (seen above) and remodelled the wings. The house had been let to tenants, Gooch and Bainbridge, before the sale. Offered again in 1915, it was afterwards the home of the Archer Ludlows who were there in about 1919 and 'gave rather good private dances'. Following purchase by a developer, Horace Brueton, who saved many trees in the park in the building of new houses, it became successively Malvern Hall Girls' School, a high school for girls and a comprehensive. Large additions are not without merit. It is now St Martin's Independent Day School for Girls and is handsomely maintained (below).

There are tales of hauntings, such as ghostly footsteps near the gateway erected by Greswold(e) Lewis in 1811, made to an old Inigo Jones design. Maybe the spirit of the Revd Charles Meysey-Wigley or unhappy Charlotte? One thing is certain, there was never a 'Malvern Hall murder'. (One Williams did shoot his innkeeper brother-in-law on the Isle of Man. . . .) The red hand which appears on heraldry in St Alphege's church is the 'Red Hand of Ulster', not a stigma on a coat of arms.

Having condemned Soane as a 'modern Goth' after the architect had removed external embellishments to the mansion, Greswold(e) Lewis used an old Inigo Jones design for the forecourt gate pillars. These remain, but minus their painted heraldry, removed by restorers. The statues of ancient warriors have unfortunately gone; one damaged by a car, the other regrettably sold some years ago.

In Sicily, Lewis and Soane visited the Villa Palagonia, near Palermo, where they would see the extraordinary carvings reputedly made by a mad monk, and the mirrored interiors. I was one day to follow in their footsteps, fascinated by the black-clad custodian who pirouetted to show me how the dancers would be reflected in the ballroom ceiling, a never-to-be-forgotten New Year experience.

In 1798 Soane sent a design for a 'Barn à la Paestum'. The author Dorothy Stroud said, 'this remarkable small building . . . originally served as a store and cart shed'. It was also an alternative entrance to Malvern Park. I vaguely picture remains of a drive across the park. It was also known as the Kennels; I believe hounds were kept there.

Broadwas Court, Broadwas-on-Teme, near Worcester, English home of Francis ('Frank') Greswolde Williams, after Bredenbury Court, Bromyard. He acquired land in Kenya, engaged in drug-running (see *White Mischief*, the book by James Fox, not the film), had a private racecourse, craved entertainment including 'music-hall' performers at Broadwas, liked fast cars and flying, taking friends on flights and depositing them miles from home. There were coloured servants at the Court, one sleeping nightly outside 'Frank's' bedroom door. He was generous, but there were devastating results if one disagreed with him. His brother, Henry, succeeded to Broadwas.

Blakesley Hall, Yardley, sixteenth century and now a prized possession of Birmingham, was built by Richard Smalbroke and was among the many properties of Henry Greswold(e) Lewis. These also included, as well as Malvern Hall, Hillfield Hall and the Manor House, Solihull, Olton Hall, the Manor House, Harbury, Radford Hall and The Cottage, Radford Semele, but he did not occupy them all! He also had a London residence. At one time a farmhouse, Blakesley was subsequently the home of an industrialist who had a magnificent collection of longcase clocks.

A memorial in the cloisters of Worcester Cathedral to 'Frank's' son Francis, a victim of the First World War. Had Malvern Hall not been sold, and had there been no war, he might well have been 'Squire' of Solihull.

Pevsner describes this memorial in Yardley Church as 'a most remarkable monument, consisting of a curtained cave containing the marble statues of the praying parson and his wife'. The Revd Henry Greswold, Rector of Solihull, and his spouse, Ann Marshall, are surrounded by medallions representing their eleven offspring, one, Humphrey, being the builder of Malvern Hall. You might call it an opera box, save that people do not usually pray in opera boxes! A Greswolde Lewis memorial nearby praises Henry's 'urbanity of manner acquired and improved by long intercourse with the best society in the capitals and courts of Europe'. It has been suggested that he wrote this himself, as he almost certainly did poor Charlotte's epitaph. The tablet provokes further speculation: did he, as stated in West's Warwickshire directory of c. 1830, ever really erect the obelisk – allegedly 180 feet high – commemorating the Battle of Waterloo? This would have terminated the lime avenue which is now largely Brueton Avenue. More mysteriously, an early nineteenth-century cartographer indicates avenues fore and aft of Malvern Hall, each with an obelisk!

Old Berry Hall would appear to be late fifteenth or early sixteenth century, is partly moated (sign of an earlier house) and was reduced in size years ago. Said to be haunted by a 'friendly' ghost, it was from 1505 the seat of the prominent Warings, who gave their name to Warings Green, Tanworth, and a prioress to Henwood nunnery. When Charles Waring died in 1671 it passed to his daughter, Mary, whose husband William outlived her and died in 1718, when it became a farmhouse. Grandly timbered, with later brick chimneys, it is a gem, ironically outliving the 'new' Hall. Remarkable features are the jutting garderobes, sometimes mistaken for powder-closets, but really serving a more useful purpose linked with overflow to the moat. The Old Hall was formerly part of the Gillott, Upton and Tippetts estate, but is now separately owned and carefully restored, in most excellent hands. The Victorian photograph shows part of the central doorway, removed from the original position which would be under the gable.

Neo-Tudor Berry Hall, designed in about 1870 by J.A. Chatwin, who also submitted an Italianate design, was built for Joseph Gillott, son of the founder of the penmaking firm. In 1904, following the death of its owner, the extensive estate was sold, but his son, also Joseph, lived on at the Hall for a few years. It was then bought by Mrs William Upton of Sutton Grange, Solihull. In 1908 her husband accidentally shot himself on the front doorstep. (The inquest was reported in the *Warwick & Warwickshire Advertiser,* 12 September). Mrs Upton afterwards married Maurice Davis, the Birmingham antique dealer. The house, later the home of the Tippetts family, from 1939, is no more: gone are the imposing main staircase, the tower based on Tom Tower, at Christ Church, Oxford, woodcarving by Lamb of Manchester and stained glass by Hardman of Birmingham. Where is the chimney-piece reputedly from Kenilworth Castle? The extensive arboretum — another Westonbirt — cries out for restoration, but does have a tree preservation order on it. One dreams of the glass-houses with delicious fruit, and bougainvillea, the camomile lawn. The gates of the impressive main drive, with Gillott pen nib on the lock, are now, I gather, in Wiltshire. A lake constructed by my father's workmen remains; my sister-in-law, Mrs E.P. Lines (née Hemming) remembers swimming there.

In August 1980 a Birmingham newspaper reported that plans had been drawn up to convert Berry Hall into a luxury hotel. By this time floors and roof had caved in. The plan was first recommended then refused by Solihull and West Midlands county councillors. Nothing of the building now remains.

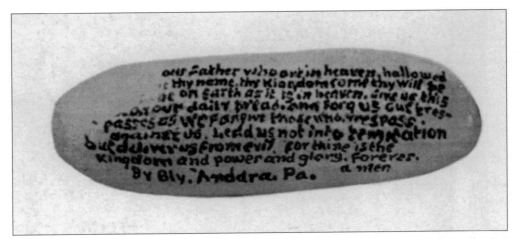

Described as 'a unique example of penmanship', this shows the Lord's Prayer 'written on one side of an actual grain of rice with a Gillott's No. 2000 Superfine pointed pen . . . the original being in the possession of Joseph Gillott & Sons'. The factory, in Graham Street, Birmingham, closed in 1945.

Berry Hall's builder Joseph Gillott married Maria Sault, a pretty girl from his factory. She was sent away to be educated and to acquire the social graces which she did with aplomb, becoming very popular locally, prior to premature death. Unfortunately, bringing up a family was not one of her greatest accomplishments, with some dire results.

On walks with Father, Henwood Mill, with its pigeon-cotes, always delighted me. Sold in 1904 as part of the Berry Hall estate, it stands on the site of the mill belonging to Henwood Priory, and served last century both as mill and bakery.

Father inspecting one of his cottages with Spot. Some cottages were let at about 5s a week, but had no bathroom, only a tin bath which hung on the wall of an outhouse when not in use.

My great uncle, Abraham Stowe, expert nurseryman, lived in his last years at this probably early nineteenth-century house, at the junction of Lugtrout Lane and Wherrett's Well Lane, earlier at Stonehurst nearby, adjoining Cox's timber yard. The rather ecclesiastical character is charming, with a little tower and mock bell turret.

OLTON MILL.

Olton Mill. The watermill survived a windmill but
has now disappeared, replaced by modern homes;
only the millpool on the far side of Lode Lane is left
for us. I remember disused millstones on a grassy
bank and the house occupied by the Cotons. 'Ernie'
Coton could sow a whole field for my brother by
hand, in unerringly straight lines (even if slightly
lubricated), and was a tremendous character.

Caroline Meysey Wigley (1801–73) by
Theophilus Clive. She inherited Olton Hall
from her short-lived brother, Edmund, of
Malvern Hall. On her marriage to the Revd
Archer Clive the house, which figures in her
diary, was let. A prominent tenant was her
relative, William Wilson, the rakish if lovable
squire of Knowle, who lost his fortune,
emigrated to America, and, returning to
England, died in poverty in London in 1887
(see *Green Peas at Christmas*, ed. G. Fleetwood
Wilson, 1924). When the Clives left Solihull
for Whitfield, Herefordshire, and after
Caroline's tragic death by fire, Olton Hall was
sold to the Alstons of Elmdon, as was Olton
Mill, and again let.

Once noted for fine panelling from Henwood and Knowle Halls, Olton Hall, old seat of the Palmers, was
partly rebuilt in about 1824, and has been replaced by a pub in a now populous district that includes the
Rover factory. The land was held by Edwin, Earl of Mercia, and later, under the Conqueror, by Cristina,
sister of Edgar the Atheling and of St Margaret of Scotland. She became a nun, retiring to Romsey Abbey.
A nearby mound, 'Hob's Moat', signifies the castle built by her successors, the de Limesis and de
Odingsells.

Dove House Farm, Dove House Lane, dates from about 1500, and was the old home of the Leas who moved to Malvern Park Farm. It has handsome timbering and rebuilding in brick. 'No traces of a dove-house now remain' (*VCH*). A nearby house, Coppice Close, had a staircase from Coombe Abbey, near Coventry.

Silhill, or Solihull, Hall (not to be confused with Silhill House) was illegally demolished overnight. Wrongly attributed to Sir William de Odingsells, lord of the manor, this house, originally moated, was bought as part of Olton Manor by sixteenth-century Richard Middlemore of Edgbaston, who married Ann Greswold of Longdon Hall. A Robert Middlemore was followed by a daughter Mary, wife of Sir John Gage, 4th baronet, their daughters Lady Shelley (later Mathew) and Viscountess Fauconberg selling to Harry Gough in 1717. After the death of Captain Richard Gough's widow, it was sold to Thomas Chattock (born in 1774) and was owned by his son, R.S. Chattock, of Northmede, in 1905. The remains of Silhill Hall were removed to the nearby airport and there interred: an irreparable loss to Solihull.

Silhill Hall had a fourteenth-century Great Hall which, though long divided, could have been restored and its grand roof exposed. This measured drawing of the great hall, by the distinguished architect J.A. Cossins, is in the possession of Birmingham Archaeological Society.

CHAPTER FIVE

PARADISE LOST

My favourite walk, partly because of family ties, was to Elmdon. One passed the Pound, already just a name signifying a one-time enclosure for straying livestock. Then allotments and Elmdon Heath cottages, soon to be joined by Greville Arms and council houses. Swingler's shop – open all hours – provided an ample penny-worth of sweets. From the Iron Bridge – still spoken of with a touch of respect as if it were only yesterday's invention – I looked into the deep canal cutting where violets and luscious blackberries grew, and there might be a painted boat and butty. Beyond Magpie Hall, the continuing Damson Lane held distant prospects of Yardley's spire and fox-haunted woodlands, and passed by Fordrove Farm and Georgian Whar Hall, with possible hum of a threshing-machine, and in the early year the inevitable patch of snowdrops.

A clapgate heralded a first view of Elmdon Hall, solid and Georgian again, though as jovial Billy Markham once said of Whar Hall, I don't think bedroom curtains there ever assumed the horizontal in a stiff wind! Then, the park drive and a sinister, yew-hung pool fronting flower and kitchen gardens. Parkland gave way to woodland screening hall and church. There was the estate carpenter's shop and the camellia-house where maids once begged flowers for their best dresses and the annual servants' ball. Rooks complained in elms around the small churchyard where more snowdrops grew. The church would be open, no thought of thieves.

Faintly, I recall Elmdon Hall – now gone as if it had never been, like the black and gilt clock on the stables – in full occupation. But usually there was just Hannah, once head housemaid with baskets for pampered cats around an enormous kitchen range, but no fine gamepie or ale for backdoor callers. Grandfather first showed me the big 'Saloon', as it was always termed, which once had heard Barber Hopkins' famous fiddle, as he pranced around the room, leading the dancing; and the ice-house that had needed an army of workmen to fill it, a task rewarded with the traditional 'Ice Supper' of boiled mutton. I would go down to the big lake, and find a ruined bath-house in the Engine Grove. There was the Terrace for estate workfolk and the tiny school, whose inmates were released to act as beaters for the Squire's shooting-party and given roast beef topped with plenty of mustard.

Save for a welcome green oasis, my 'Paradise' is lost. Massed houses, complex of roads, airport – growing ever larger, exhibitions and Rover factory have taken over, for better or worse.

Elmdon Hall (architect unknown) dated from the late eighteenth century. It was built by Abraham Spooner and his son, Isaac, the latter father-in-law of William Wilberforce, two of whose children were born there. Sold to William Charles Alston, it passed to his son, William, and then to the elder William's daughter, Mrs Elizabeth Louisa Alston-Roberts-West, being sold after her death in 1929, and the remaining contents being dispersed. During the Second World War it was a Home Guard Post, Air Raid Warning Centre and Civil Defence Workers' Club. Nothing remains of it, but part of the park with a big lake is still in existence, and is in public use. W.W. Waters bought the Hall, giving land to extend the churchyard.

Family group, 1887. Standing, right to left: J.F. Alston, 'Squire' W.C. Alston, unknown. Sitting: Mrs E.L. Roberts-West, husband J. Roberts-West, unknown lady standing. Mrs Roberts-West, subsequently Alston-Roberts-West, had two sisters, Mrs Cradock-Hartopp (d. 1923) and Mrs Smythe (died 1927), daughter-in-law of Rector Smythe of Solihull.

'Squire' William Charles Alston (died in 1917) inherited Elmdon Hall from his father. High Sheriff of Warwickshire, 1884, he served as a magistrate at Solihull and Coleshill and as major and Hon. Lieutenant Colonel of the Warwickshire Yeomanry. A bachelor, the 'Squire' was renowned for his feudal hospitality, a glass-sided private 'omnibus' carrying guests from local railway stations for his 'shoots,' the Elmdon coverts famed for pheasants and the Sheldon estate for hares. A fine game shot himself, as well as golfer, he was also noted as a cricketer in his younger days. Having lost an eye (shooting?), he kept a boxful of glass eyes. Here he is with Frank, the keeper, and Ruby.

Judging from a family album at Alscot Park, James Fetherston Alston, the 'Squire's' brother (their mother a Fetherston of Packwood House) was very fond of cycling, doubtless avoiding the opprobrium bestowed on my parents! (The monkey by the right-hand wheel was apparently stuffed, but I don't know why it appeared on this photograph.) The brothers were regular members of 'the old-time Warwickshire cricket eleven; indeed many of their county matches were played in Elmdon Park,' said the *Birmingham Post* in 1917.

James's father had thoughts of ordination for him; he became Corresponding Manager for Elmdon School, but not Vicar of Hampton-in-Arden as envisaged. However, a humble boy on the estate was sent to school, and duly ordained. He preached in Elmdon Church, although his mother declared that she 'would rather have seen him at the ploughtail'. Another lad, again a widow's son, became a dental surgeon thanks to the Alstons, who earned the reputation of being among the 'good families', caring for their dependants. Others were helped; a burglar was caught and imprisoned, but the 'Squire' afterwards gave him a job; his gratitude took the form of a model ship he had made, long preserved at Elmdon Hall. Just recollected is one of the red cloaks given to Elmdon girls, but not the plum-coloured coats provided for the old men. A well-spiced rice pudding was served to children after the morning service at the church, but I'm not sure if this emanated from Hall or Rectory.

Abraham Spooner, who lived to be about ninety-eight, built St Nicholas' church, Elmdon, completed in 1781. It replaced a church with timbered tower. The picture shows the church before Second World War enlargement to meet the demands of a much bigger congregation, when it was found that the existing structure was by no means as solid as long thought!

The interior of St Nicholas' church before alterations and extension. In the early days of the Alstons, the family walked in procession to church, headed by a black retriever. The dog curled himself up before the fire in the pew in the top right-hand corner. Candle-light was a great incentive for one's walk under the stars on a winter's morning, but this photograph shows electric light installed.

The Revd Harrison Goodenough Hayter (died in 1934) married in 1884 Alice Margarette (died in 1937), daughter of the Hon. and Revd Henry Pitt Cholmondeley. She and her sister, Mary, Lady Mordaunt, of Walton Hall, Wellesbourne, had two peers, Lords Leigh and Delamere, as grandparents. Aristocratic, dress hardly seems to have worried Mrs Hayter. Wearing a cloak made from one of her husband's old cassocks, she was approached in Elmdon Park by a tramp, who looked at her pityingly, pointed to the Rectory and warned, 'You won't get anything there, mum!' Actually, food was generously bestowed, but no money. Appearance at the little school, also in the park, where she taught Scripture, was apt to alarm new pupils, dark clothes, dark glasses, and big hat making them think the good lady was a crow.

Today there is a roar of planes over the Hayters' Georgian rectory, which no longer serves its original purpose. The neighbouring school and the terrace have vanished, like the Hall, but a temple-like lodge survives beside the Birmingham to Coventry road.

'The house of Francis Hoby commonly called the Sign of the Cock,' as the seventeenth-century inn was known in 1672. Did anyone preserve the sign, or the stone eagles on the nearby Elmdon Hall gates, remarkably similar to those outside a certain Oxfordshire airfield? Elmdon in wartime housed the RAF.

My great-great-grandfather, Josiah Limbrey (or Limbery), hailed from Dorset and was landlord last century of the Cock, as well as Elmdon village postmaster and farmer. An ancestor narrowly escaped fame, or premature death; master of a coasting vessel, he agreed to take the hunted Charles II from Charmouth to France, but his worried wife locked him in his bedroom. Charles waited in vain.

This photograph shows the demolition of the Cock Inn in progress.

ACKNOWLEDGEMENTS

My grateful thanks are due to Mrs S. Bates, Local History Librarian, Solihull Central Library and the staff of the Local History Department, The Duke of Westminster, The Lady Mary Clive, Dame Barbara Cartland, Mrs J. Alston-Roberts-West, Mrs E.P. Lines, Miss M. Lines, Mrs E.J. Walsh, B. Gallagher, Mrs D. Mason, J.P. Price, the Revd B. Boyle, D.R. Patterson, R.A. Cohen, G.C. Burman, R. Griswold, M. Bryant, Mrs M. Jewsbury, the Chase family, R. Handford, Ruckleigh School (D. Cooper-Smith), G.A. Davison, R.A. Davies, S.T. Budd, S. Foster, Mrs E.G. Handley, Mrs B. Simmonds, D.J.N. Green, J.E. Goodchild, Mrs M. Crowley, V. Bird, Dr D. Gray, all at Sutton Publishing, Warwick County Record Office (R. Chamberlaine Brothers), Royal Leamington Spa Library (G. Archer), Royal Birmingham Society of Artists (R. Forbes, Curator), Birmingham Central Library, Birmingham Art Gallery, Solihull Society of Arts, Solihull Photographic Society, Royal Bank of Scotland, Solihull, Lloyds Bank, Solihull, Weston Park Enterprises Ltd, the Shakespeare Birthplace Trust, Solihull College of Technology, Lionel Photography, Solihull, St Alphege's church, Elmdon, Olton and Shirley churches, St Augustine of England RC Church, Solihull, Christ Church, Solihull, Sacred Heart RC Church, Droitwich. Also the late Sir John Betjeman, J. Burman, G. Lines, Mrs A.L.S. Lines, W.F. Lines, Mrs L. Titmus, J. Titmus, Mrs S. Garfield, Miss M. Mitchell, Miss F.A. Barrows, C. Godson, Miss D. Lea, Mrs M. Larner, Mrs L. Pegg, V.G. Pegg, D.P.H. Jewsbury, Dr J. Jelley, Mrs M. Beresford.

Every endeavour has been made to trace the copyright holders or owners of photographs, but in some cases this has proved impossible.

BIBLIOGRAPHY

Bates, Sue, *Solihull: A Pictorial History*, 1991
Burman, John, *In the Forest of Arden*, 1948
——, *Solihull and its School*, 1939
——, *The Burman Chronicle*, 1940
Bloom, Ursula, *Edwardian Daydream*, 1972
Clive, Mary (ed.), *Caroline Clive*, 1949
Dugdale, Sir William, *The Antiquities of Warwickshire*, 1656
Handley, E.G. (ed.), *Travelling On. The Continuing Story of Methodism in Solihull*, 1997
Hey, Colin G., *The Warwickshire Coterie*, 1991
Lines, Charles, *Coughton Court and the Throckmorton Story*
——, *Weston Park and the Earls of Bedford*

Malley, Bernard, *Solihull and the Catholic Faith*, 1939
Pemberton, R., *Solihull and its Church*, 1905
Solihull News
Solihull Parish Magazine, 'Solihull from 1836 onwards', 1933–4
Solihull Times
Stroud, Dorothy, *Sir John Soane, Architect*, 1996
The *Birmingham Post*
Victoria County History of Warwickshire, vol. 4, 1947
Wart, Irving van der, *Souvenir of Old England by an Anglo-American*, 1880
Woodall, Joy, *The Book of Greater Solihull*, 1990

BRITAIN IN OLD PHOTOGRAPHS

SUTTON'S PHOTOGRAPHIC HISTORY OF TRANSPORT